WILLIAM PENN

OVERCOMING ADVERSITY

WILLIAM PENN

Rebecca Stefoff

Introduction by James Scott Brady,
Trustee, the Center to Prevent Handgun Violence
Vice Chairman, the Brain Injury Foundation

Chelsea House Publishers
Philadelphia

Cover: Penn: Archive Photos; Letter: Corbis-Bettman; City Hall: © Judy L. Hasday.

Frontis: A bronze sculpture of William Penn watches over the city of Philadelphia.

CHELSEA HOUSE PUBLISHERS

EDITORIAL DIRECTOR Stephen Reginald
PRODUCTION MANAGER Pamela Loos
MANAGING EDITOR Jim Gallagher
PICTURE EDITOR Judy Hasday
ART DIRECTOR Sara Davis
SENIOR PRODUCTION EDITOR Lisa Chippendale

Staff for **William Penn**
SENIOR EDITOR Therese De Angelis
ASSOCIATE ART DIRECTOR Takeshi Takahashi
DESIGNER Keith Trego
PICTURE RESEARCHER Patricia Burns
COVER DESIGN Keith Trego

First Printing

1 3 5 7 9 8 6 4 2

Library of Congress Cataloging-in-Publication Data

Stefoff, Rebecca, 1951-
William Penn / Rebecca Stefoff.

112 pp. cm. — (Overcoming adversity)
Includes bibliographical references and index.
Summary: Focuses on the struggles of the founder of Pennsylvania who promoted the Quaker religion and spent his lifetime preaching the right of each individual to choose his own faith.

ISBN 0-7910-4873-X — ISBN 0-7910-4874-8 (pbk.)
1. Penn, William, 1644-1718—Juvenile literature. 2. Pioneers—Pennsylvania—Biography—Juvenile literature. 3. Quakers—Pennsylvania—Biography—Juvenile literature. 4. Pennsylvania—History—Colonial period, ca. 1600-1775—Juvenile literature. [1. Penn, William, 1644-1718. 2. Pioneers. 3. Quakers. 4. Pennsylvania—History—Colonial period, ca. 1600-1775.]
I. Title. II. Series.
F152.2.S85 1997
974.8'02'092—dc21   97-23998
[B]   CIP
                                                                 AC

CONTENTS

On Facing Adversity *James Scott Brady*   7

1 A Prisoner of Conscience   11

2 Born into Troubled Times   19

3 The Young Seeker   35

4 Ireland and the Quakers   47

5 Trials   59

6 The Holy Experiment   71

7 The Proprietor of Penn's Woods   85

8 Penn's Legacy   97

Appendix   105

Further Reading   107

Chronology   108

Index   110

OVERCOMING ADVERSITY

TIM ALLEN
comedian/performer

JIM CARREY
comedian/performer

BILL CLINTON
U.S. President

JAMES EARL JONES
actor

ABRAHAM AND MARY LINCOLN
political family

WILLIAM PENN
Pennsylvania's founder

ROSEANNE
entertainer

ON FACING ADVERSITY

James Scott Brady

I guess it's a long way from a Centralia, IL, train yard to the George Washington University Hospital Trauma Unit. My dad was a yardmaster for the old Chicago, Burlington & Quincy Railroad. As a child, I used to get to sit in the engineer's lap and imagine what it was like to drive that train. I guess I always have liked being in the "driver's seat."

Years later, however, my interest turned from driving trains to driving campaigns. In 1979, former Texas governor John Connally hired me as a press secretary in his campaign for the American presidency. We lost the Republican primary to a former Hollywood star named Ronald Reagan. But I managed to jump over to the Reagan campaign. When Reagan was elected in 1980, I was "sitting in the catbird seat," as humorist James Thurber would say—poised to be named presidential press secretary. I held that title throughout the eight years of the Reagan administration. But not without one terrible, extended interruption.

It happened barely two months after the Reagan administration took office. I never even heard the shots. On March 30, 1981, my life went blank in an instant. In an attempt to assassinate President Reagan, John Hinckley Jr. armed himself with a "Saturday Night Special"—a low quality, $29 pistol—and shot wildly as our presidential entourage exited a Washington hotel. One of the exploding bullets struck me just above the left eye. It shattered into a couple dozen fragments, some of which penetrated my skull and entered my brain.

The next few months of my life were a nightmare of repeated surgery, broken contact with the outside world, and a variety of medical complications. More than once, I was very close to death.

The next few years were filled with frustrating struggles to function with a paralyzed right side, struggles to speak and communicate.

To people who face and defeat daunting obstacles, "ambition" is not becoming wealthy or famous or winning elections or awards. Words like "ambition" and "achievement" and "success" take on very different meanings. The objective is just to live, to wake up every morning. The goals are not lofty; they are very ordinary.

My own heroes are ordinary folks—but they accomplish extraordinary things because they try. My greatest hero is my wife, Sarah. She's accomplished a lot of things in life, but two stand out. The first has been the way she has cared for me and our son since I was shot. A tremendous tragedy and burden was dropped unexpectedly into her life, totally beyond her control and without justification. She could have given up; instead, she focused her energies on preserving our family and returning our lives to normal as much as possible. Week by week, month by month, year by year, she has not reached for the miraculous, just for the normal. Yet in focusing on the normal, she has helped accomplish the miraculous.

Her other most remarkable accomplishment, to me, has been spearheading the effort to keep guns out of the hands of criminals and children in America. Opponents call her a "gun grabber"; I call her a national hero. And I am not alone.

After a seven-year battle, during which Sarah and I worked tirelessly to educate the public about the need for stronger gun laws, the Brady Bill became law in 1993. It was a victory, achieved in the face of tremendous opposition, that now benefits all Americans. Since the law has been in effect, background checks have stopped 173,000 criminals and other high-risk purchasers from buying handguns, and the law has helped to reduce illegal gun trafficking.

Sarah was not pursuing fame, or even recognition. She simply started at one point—when our son, Scott, found a loaded handgun on the seat of a pickup truck and, thinking it was a toy, pointed it at Sarah.

Fortunately, no one was hurt. But seeing a gun nearly bring a second tragedy upon our family, Sarah became determined to do whatever she could to prevent senseless death and injury from guns.

Some people think of Sarah as a powerful political force. To me, she's the person who so many times fed me and helped me dress during my long years of recovery.

Overcoming obstacles is part of life, not just for people who are challenged by disabilities, illnesses, or tragedies, but for all people. No matter what the obstacle—fear, disability, prejudice, grief, or a difficulty that isn't likely to "just go away"—we can all work to make this world a better place.

In 17th-century England, the Friends—or Quakers—were viewed as a threat to the government and were forced to meet in secret, as this 19th-century photogravure shows. William Penn is portrayed in the center left.

1

A PRISONER
OF CONSCIENCE

ON SEPTEMBER 3, 1667, a group of people converged on a house in
the city of Cork on the east coast of Ireland. They gathered quietly and
sat on benches and chairs in a large room. Men and women alike were
soberly dressed in dark-colored clothing that was simple and plain in
style, far removed from the extravagant frills, laces, and ruffles that
were the fashion of the time. The men wore hats, which they did not
remove when they took their places; the women wore modest head-
dresses of white cloth.

Despite their polite manners, these quiet folk were lawbreakers,
engaged in a forbidden activity. They were members of a religious
group that some people called the Quakers, although they called themselves the Friends, and they were meeting to worship in their own way:
without a priest or a preacher, without a standard service or a ritual,
without even a church. Such meetings were illegal; worshiping God
was dangerous for the Friends. The British government, which ruled
Ireland and England, had outlawed Quaker meetings as a threat to the
state. In the eyes of the king and the government, this strange new reli-

gion that failed to follow traditional practices was an insult to the established order. In 1660 and 1662 the British legislative assembly, or Parliament, had passed laws that limited the rights of the Quakers and the many other new, nontraditional religious sects that had sprung up in the 17th century. Among other restrictions, these laws made it illegal for more than five Quakers to gather together for what the 1662 act called "pretence of worship." Quakers who defied these laws could be arrested and jailed.

Some communities were more tolerant of the Quakers than others, just as some outsiders respected the Quakers—or at least ignored them—while others mocked and despised them. But although a Quaker meeting was quite likely to be untroubled, the risk of persecution was real. Hundreds of Friends had been arrested, fined, or worse; some had died in prison.

The Friends who gathered in Cork that September day were from many walks of life. Among them were laborers, shopkeepers, and merchants. But one of them came from a different class of society altogether. He was a 22-year-old Englishman named William Penn. His garments were of richer material and were more stylishly cut than those of the other people in the room, and at his hip he wore a sword—something permitted only to the gentlemen of the upper classes.

Young Penn was indeed a gentleman. His father, who owned a large estate near Cork, was an admiral of the British fleet, a war hero, and a friend of King Charles II of England; the young man himself was on friendly terms with the king. William Penn had been brought up by his affectionate but strict father to have a place in court life. He was expected to behave as a traditional English aristocrat should, not to mingle with suspicious religious minorities in outlawed meetings. Yet unknown to Admiral Penn, William had been attending Quaker meetings for half a year. So far he had encountered no trouble, no harassment. But this gathering was different.

The simple, dark-colored clothing and modest headgear of the Friends stood in stark contrast to the frilly, colorful fashions of the 17th century.

A meeting of Friends was unlike the traditional Church of England services that Penn had attended throughout his childhood, the services of other Protestant sects such as Lutherans and Puritans, or the Roman Catholic Mass. The Friends were Christians who believed that God speaks directly to each individual, without need of a special building or a hierarchy of priests and church officials to interpret God's word. All anyone has to do to receive God's message is read the Bible and meditate or pray. Thus

Quaker meetings were sometimes completely silent, as each Friend's thoughts turned inward. Anyone who wished to speak could stand and do so at any time, and speakers often shared their thoughts or experiences, but meetings tended to be tranquil affairs.

The serenity of the September 3 meeting was suddenly broken by clattering footsteps on the stairs. A soldier, loud and ill-mannered and possibly the worse for drink, burst into the room and began bullying the humble Quakers. The soldier felt confident that no Quaker would challenge him, for the Friends honored peace above all things—to be a Friend was to reject all forms of violence, even in self-defense. But William Penn had been brought up with an aristocrat's touchy pride, and he was outraged at such insulting behavior from a common ruffian. He jumped from his seat and advanced on the soldier. One account of the incident says that Penn laid his hand on the hilt of his sword; another version says that Penn grabbed the man by his collar and prepared to kick him downstairs. But before he could act, the horrified Quakers urged him not to commit violence.

Penn now faced his first test as a Quaker. Should he follow the instincts of his upper-class, military background and give the ill-mannered soldier a well-deserved thrashing, or should he follow the Quaker principles that he had recently adopted? After a moment of hesitation, he released his grip on the soldier and let the fellow go. The angry soldier rushed off. In choosing the path of nonviolence, Penn had passed the test of his principles. But another test soon followed.

The soldier returned with a squad of constables and other soldiers. Everyone in the house was arrested and hauled before the mayor of Cork, who was uncomfortably surprised to recognize the son of Sir William Penn in the crowd of prisoners. Hoping to avoid the embarrassment of throwing a lord's son into jail, the mayor announced that Penn had obviously been arrested by mistake, as he

Penn's 1667 letter to the earl of Orrery introduced the concept of separation of church and state. This idea became one of the founding principles of the United States Constitution when the Bill of Rights (shown here)—the first ten amendments to the Constitution—was adopted in 1791.

could not possibly be a Quaker. He added that Penn was free to go.

This was Penn's second test, and he passed it without hesitation. Stepping from the prisoner's dock to the mayor's bench, he said loudly and clearly that there had been no mistake. He was a Quaker.

Penn then insisted upon being charged with the same crimes as the other Quakers. He said that because he had studied law, he would defend himself and his fellow Quakers against the charges. And by the way, he asked the flustered mayor, just what were those charges?

The mayor responded that the Quakers were charged with rioting and holding an unlawful assembly under the 1660 law. Penn argued that the true purpose of that law had been to protect the state not against Quakers but against another new sect called the Fifth Monarchists, whose religious beliefs were linked to plans to overthrow the English government. The Quakers posed no such danger, he explained, and therefore should be exempt from the law.

Such subtle reasoning was beyond the mayor. He ordered all the Quakers, including Penn, thrown into jail. Legend says that Penn paused at the door of the jail, unbuckled his jeweled sword, and handed it to a puzzled but grateful bystander, announcing that he had given up fighting forever. No evidence supports this persistent story, but perhaps it is true; other events in Penn's life suggest that he was capable of grand, impulsive gestures.

Once he and his fellow Friends were in jail, Penn's first action was to send for pen, ink, and paper. He wrote a letter to the earl of Orrery, who was the president of Munster, the part of Ireland where Cork is located. The earl could overrule the mayor's decision to jail the Quakers—and he also happened to be a friend of Penn's father.

This letter was the first of many documents that Penn was to write about an issue that became the central focus of his life: freedom of religion. Instead of simply pleading for justice for himself and his friends, he called for tolerance toward all religions. He declared that a person's relationship with God should be regulated not by kings or mayors but by the individual's own conscience, and he wrote defiantly, "Religion, which is at once my crime and my innocence, makes me a prisoner to the Mayor's malice, but mine own free man." Penn reminded Orrery that the Quakers were nonviolent and posed no political threat. Then he went a step further, suggesting that the state had no right to favor one religious sect over another. This idea—that church and state should be separate—was considered extremely unsound and dangerous in 1667. Later it was to become one of the founding principles of the United States Constitution.

Whether or not Orrery was impressed with Penn's plea for liberty and toleration is unknown. Perhaps he simply wanted to get his friend's son out of prison. Whatever the reason, however, he ordered that Penn and the other 18 Quaker prisoners be set free. William Penn's experience in Cork was the first time that he was jailed for his beliefs, but it would not be the last. Only a few years later he would be considered a dangerous political prisoner and thrown into solitary confinement in the notorious Tower of London.

Penn would suffer other hardships as well, including money problems, betrayals by friends, and stormy relationships with his father and with his own sons. Yet he would also experience great successes: triumphs of the spirit, if not always worldly glories. He would win respect for his courage as a spokesperson for the Quakers. He would become the owner of the largest private property ever possessed by anyone not of royal blood. And he would have the rare privilege of turning his dreams into reality by founding the colony of Pennsylvania.

But while Penn is often remembered simply as the founder of Pennsylvania, he was much more than that. He was one of the first thinkers to ponder deeply the question of individual rights and to speak and write on behalf of those rights. In Britain and throughout Europe, he fought against injustice and prejudice. His long crusade for religious toleration helped change the laws of Britain, bringing greater liberty of conscience to all. Long after his death, his beliefs and practices helped shape the new nation of which Pennsylvania became a part.

The Penn family crest, with the motto "Dum Clavum Teneam" ("As long as I hold the helm"), a fitting phrase for a family of sea merchants.

2

BORN INTO
TROUBLED TIMES

THROUGHOUT HIS LIFE, the founder of Pennsylvania was proud of his ancestry. The Penn family name was an old and honorable one in England. Although William Penn claimed to be related to a family named Penn in the county of Buckinghamshire that could trace its ancestry to a Norman knight of the 11th century, genealogists—historians who specialize in the study of family trees—have not been able to prove a connection between the Buckinghamshire Penns and the founder's own family.

The Quaker William Penn's family can, however, be traced several generations back to a prosperous farmer, also named William Penn, who owned a large estate in Gloucestershire, a county in central England. This ancestral Penn died in 1591. His son, another William, was a law clerk. Among the law clerk's six children was a son named Giles, who became a merchant sea captain. Sailing out of Bristol, a trade port on England's southwest coast, Giles Penn made himself into an important personage. He traded with the Spanish, Moroccan, and Algerian merchants and pirates who controlled the western part of the Mediterranean Sea, and because he learned Arabic and made friends among the Moors and Algerians, he was able to obtain Arabian horses and hunting falcons, which were highly prized throughout Europe. By making gifts of these horses and falcons to members of the English aristocracy, Giles Penn gained influence at court. He was appointed to the post of English consul, or diplomatic representative, in the Moroccan city of Salé. One of his principal duties was ransoming English captives who had fallen into the hands of Arab pirates.

Giles Penn planned a lucrative career in commerce for his sons, George and William. But George, who had married a Spanish woman, fell afoul of the Spanish authorities for unknown reasons and was thrown into prison in Seville. He was eventually released, but he was ordered never to return to Spain; this ruined Giles Penn's hopes of a family trading company with branches in Spain and England. Giles's other son, William, was the father of William Penn the Quaker. Giles Penn had meant for this son, who at an early age was an experienced seaman, to captain the merchant vessel that was to make the family's fortune. William Penn's career took a different direction, however. He chose a military rather than a mercantile career.

The mid-17th century was a time of great turmoil in England. Certain factions of the public grew increasingly dissatisfied with the rule of King Charles I, who had ascended the throne in 1625. Many people, particularly the officers and soldiers of the country's army, were beginning to feel that the king had too much power and that England's Parliament should have a greater say in running the country. A rift developed between the monarchists, or Royalists—who supported the absolute rights of the monarch—and the antimonarchists, or Parliamentarians—who favored reducing the king's powers and strengthening those of Parliament.

Religion and politics were closely intertwined in the 17th century, and religious differences played a great part in the upheavals of English government and society that occurred in the middle of the century. The Church of England (also called the Anglican Church) had been the country's official religion since the early 16th century. There were some Roman Catholics in England, but they were regarded with distrust and were often persecuted, as were Presbyterians. Also persecuted were the members of new Protestant sects outside the Anglican Church: these individuals were labeled Separatists, Nonconformists, or Dissenters because they declared their faiths to be separate from the officially recognized church, because they failed to conform to Anglican practices, or because they dissented from—that is, disagreed with—Anglican doctrine.

Even within the Church of England, however, there were factions. One group of Anglicans, called the Puritans, wanted to change, or purify, the church from within. The Puritans called for an end to practices that resembled those of Roman Catholics—for example, they felt that the system of bishops and archbishops should be abolished. They felt that the church, like society in general, had become preoccupied with showy, superficial effects and had lost sight of simple godliness. Eventually some Puritans, unable to come to agreement with the mainstream of the Anglican Church, fled the country; among these were the first settlers of the Massachusetts colony in North America. Other Puritans eventually left the ranks of the Anglicans and joined the Nonconformists. But the Puritan movement within the Church of England remained strong, and over time the Puritan and Parliamentarian causes became linked, largely because the king and the aristocracy were vigorously opposed to the idea of Puritan reforms. Most Puritans were Parliamentarians, and many Parliamentarians were Puritans. Thus the war between the Royalists and the Parliamentarians was partly a religious controversy.

War in England was preceded by strife in Scotland and Ireland, both of which had come under English rule. Pres-

Penn's father, Admiral Sir William Penn. Like that of his son, Sir William's loyalty to the British government was questioned on several occasions, and he was jailed under suspicion of plotting against those in power.

byterianism had been the religion of Scotland for two centuries, yet Charles I tried to force the Scots to adopt Church of England practices. At the same time, unrest broke out in Ireland, where Roman Catholicism was the dominant religion. The Irish resented the land-grabbing dominance of the English. When in 1642 a clash between King Charles and Parliament broke out into open civil war, the Irish sided with the king and the Scots sided with Parliament. The parliamentary soldiers, most of whom were Puritans, were nicknamed Roundheads because they wore their hair cropped short. Royalist forces continued to favor the long, curled hair and wigs that had been fashionable under King Charles; they were called Cavaliers. Led by a Puritan general named Oliver Cromwell, the Roundheads quickly took control of London. Before long, they had the Cavaliers on the run.

Around this time, Giles Penn's son William joined the navy. Various accounts exist about how his naval career began. Some say he joined the Royal Navy in 1641, while the king was still in power, hoping for advancement because his father stood high in the court's favor. Others say he joined in 1642, after the king had lost control of London and the navy to Parliament. In any case, William Penn's private sympathies were with the Royalists, and historians have debated his motives for serving the Parliamentarians. One possibility is that he felt a duty to remain in the navy so that he could serve his country regardless of who ruled it. Another, less idealistic, explanation is that he saw how quickly the Parliamentarians won the upper hand and decided it would be wise to stay on good terms with the party in power. At any rate, William Penn was 22 years old when the English Civil War broke out. The Parliamentarians seemed to have had no doubts about his loyalty: almost at once he was given command of a ship in the parliamentary navy. His vessel, the *Fellowship*, was part of a squadron sent to patrol the waters off Ireland to keep the rebellious Irish Catholics from sending aid to the Royalists.

Captain Penn returned to London whenever he had shore leave, and there, in 1643, he met a young widow named Margaret Jasper Vanderschuren, whose background remains something of a mystery. She came from a Protestant family of English, Irish, or Dutch origin, and she had been brought up in Rotterdam in the Netherlands. While still a teenager, she had married a Dutch merchant named Nicasius Vanderschuren, who took her to live in Ireland. It is unknown whether they had children, although it is unlikely; there is no mention in the Penn family records of any children by Margaret's first husband. Nor is it known when or how Margaret's first husband died. We

The 19th-century French artist Paul Delaroche created this dramatic and fictional scene of Oliver Cromwell surveying the body of Charles I. The execution of Charles I sent most Royalists into exile, where they plotted to defeat Cromwell.

After Margaret Penn, William's mother, lost her family's Irish property to the Royalists during the 1641 rebellion, Admiral Penn was granted this property in County Cork, Ireland, as compensation. The Penns moved to Macroom Castle, shown here, in 1657.

do know that by late 1641, when the Catholic uprising broke out in Ireland, Margaret was a widow. She fled to London with her parents to escape the turmoil in Ireland. Still quite young and by all accounts a lively, merry, good-natured woman, she soon caught the eye of Captain Penn. They were married in June 1643.

The Penns rented lodgings on Tower Hill, a fashionable neighborhood almost in the shadow of the state prison called the Tower of London. On October 14, 1644, their first child was born. They named the boy William. Although Captain Penn's ship was already on its way to Ireland, the captain himself had remained behind to be present at the child's birth. As soon as the boy was baptized—at a small, medieval church called All Hallows Barking on Tower Hill—Captain Penn took to his horse and galloped off to rejoin his ship, which had stopped along the coast. He would not return home for more than a year.

Throughout young William's childhood, in fact, his father was away at sea, except for brief visits home. The elder Penn rose to the rank of admiral, but he was plagued by troubles. While on duty in Ireland, he became friendly with an aristocrat named Lord Broghill, who was known to sympathize with the Royalists. This friendship made Cromwell and the Puritans start to question Penn's loyalty to the parliamentary government. In 1648 Penn was thrown into jail under suspicion of being a Royalist plotter. Nothing was proved against him, however, and Cromwell, who knew that the navy could not afford to lose one of its best commanders, ordered him released within a month. But rumors about Admiral Penn persisted. Some of his enemies whispered that he had Royalist leanings; others claimed that he lacked courage, drank too much, or diverted into his own pocket some of the money he was given to buy food and other supplies for the men in his command. Admiral Penn later became a war hero, but these rumors haunted him throughout his naval career.

The admiral's fortunes rose steadily for a few years, during which England continued to be shaken by momentous events. The most dramatic of these events occurred in January 1649, when Charles I, who had been captured by the Puritan forces sometime earlier, was beheaded by order of Parliament. At a time when monarchs were thought to be almost godlike and many people still believed that the touch of a royal hand could cure illness, Charles's execution was an earthshaking deed. It outraged the Royalists, of course, but even some people who had supported the Parliamentarians began to feel that the zealous Puritans had gone too far. Many Royalists, including most of the surviving Cavaliers, fled England for the Netherlands. While in exile there, they set up a court with Charles II, son of the murdered king, as its head, and they began brewing plots to defeat Cromwell.

For the time being, though, the Puritans were firmly in power in England and Cromwell was in charge. After the king was beheaded, England was declared to be a new nation, the Commonwealth, with Cromwell as its leader. A few years later Cromwell took the title Lord Protector of the Commonwealth. One of his main goals was to strengthen England against its enemies abroad—both foreign forces and exiled Royalists. Admiral Penn proved useful in this task. He scourged the Irish coast, pursued fleeing Royalist vessels into the Mediterranean, and went to battle at sea against the Dutch fleet when war broke out between England and the Netherlands in 1653. The commander of the Dutch fleet, Admiral van Tromp, fastened a broom to the highest mast of his flagship, vowing to "sweep the English from the sea." But it was the Dutch who were mopped up, and much of the credit went to Penn, whose men grappled van Tromp's own ship and tore the hated broom from the mast. Penn was rewarded with a gold chain from the lord protector.

Finding himself high in Cromwell's favor, Penn asked for a grant of land to make up for the loss of his wife's Irish property, which had been seized by the Royalists. The Puritans in turn had confiscated some Royalist lands in Ireland, and Cromwell gave Penn a parcel of it—an estate called Macroom, located near Cork. Cromwell also appointed Penn to command a fleet that was being sent to capture the Spanish colony of Hispaniola in the Caribbean Sea (the island that today is divided between the nations of Haiti and the Dominican Republic).

While Admiral Penn was making a name for himself on the high seas, his son, William, lived a quiet life at home. The Penns no longer lived in crowded, dirty London. Admiral Penn thought London was too unhealthful for his family, especially after young William suffered an attack of smallpox that caused all his hair to fall out. So the admiral had moved his wife and son and their servants to a residence near the village of Wanstead, 11 miles from London. The Wanstead home was really a farm, large enough to produce its own supply of vegetables, dairy goods, and

livestock; these were valuable considerations because the war had disrupted farming throughout the land and provisions were in short supply in London and elsewhere. The move from the city to the green, open country of Wanstead made a powerful and favorable impression on young William, who became a passionate gardener in later life and always maintained that country life was far superior to city life. "The Country is both the Philosopher's garden and his Library, in which he Reads and Contemplates the Power, Wisdom, and Goodness of God," William would write in 1693.

William later claimed that he had never wasted time in playing, and indeed it seems as though his childhood was rather earnest. Popular activities such as sports, plays,

The Chigwell Free Grammar School in Chigwell, County Essex, where young William studied until the family's move to Macroom Castle in Ireland.

fairs, and circuses had been outlawed by the Puritans, who viewed them as worldly frivolities. Rowdy games and pastimes were frowned upon. Children were expected to be serious little people and to spend all their time studying, working, or praying. And although Margaret Penn was a fun-loving woman who was far from strict, William seems to have been a naturally quiet and studious child. His only known recreation was running footraces. He greatly enjoyed his father's visits home on leave; other visitors included his grandfather Jasper and his uncle George, who told hair-raising tales of his imprisonment in a Spanish dungeon. For the most part, however, the household consisted only of William and his mother until 1652, when William's sister Margaret (called Pegg) was born. Four years later the Penns had a third child, a boy they named Richard, or Dickie.

If William had friends or playmates among the Wanstead boys, they have been forgotten. But one childhood acquaintance was destined to play a significant part in William's life: a girl named Gulielma Springett, or Guli. A few months older than William, Guli lived in Wanstead with her mother and stepfather. Admiral Penn and his family knew Guli's family, including her stepbrother, Isaac Penington, who was a Quaker—probably the first that William Penn met.

Little is known about William's early education. As a youngster on Tower Hill he may have been tutored at home or in a small private academy; no record of such teaching remains. But somehow he learned to read. By the time he was 11 years old he could read and write English and Latin; he also knew a little French and Greek. William loved reading and appears to have read widely, even as a child, but historians do not believe that Admiral Penn's household contained much of a library. Perhaps William borrowed books from tutors or family friends.

William's first known formal education began when he was enrolled in the Chigwell Free Grammar School at age

11. The school was located in the village of Chigwell, about four miles from the Penns' home, and William ran back and forth between home and school six days a week. Mondays through Saturdays, classes began at six in the morning and lasted for 10 hours in summer and 8 in winter, with an hour off on Thursdays and Saturdays to play. Chigwell was a private academy—there were no public schools in England. Only boys whose parents could afford to pay for tuition were able to attend. And like nearly all schools of the time, Chigwell was closely connected with the Church of England; in fact, it had been founded by an archbishop. William's school days thus included plenty of prayers and psalms along with lessons in grammar and history.

The Chigwell boys studied the writings of ancient Greeks and Romans whose works were considered sober and virtuous. Modern English writers—including the playwright William Shakespeare—were banned as vulgar and bawdy. All lessons were taught in Latin, and the pupils were supposed to answer questions and give recitations in Latin as well. Any boy who slipped up and spoke English in class was whipped by the schoolmaster. This rigorous program appealed to young William—or at least he said years later that it had. He described himself as being "of a retired temper" and claimed that he "could never join" in his classmates' games and pranks. His closest friend at Chigwell was the Latin teacher. At this time, William was also becoming interested in religion. He spent many hours alone reading his Bible, and he also read books and pamphlets by churchmen. He even came across some of the works of John Saltmarsh, a religious mystic who had once lived in Wanstead. Saltmarsh had written several booklets calling for religious liberty. In letters written a few years later, between 1668 and 1674, William said that in 1656 or 1657, while reading his Bible and Saltmarsh's essays, he was sometimes filled with a great sense of peace and holiness: "The Lord appeared to me," he explained. He entered

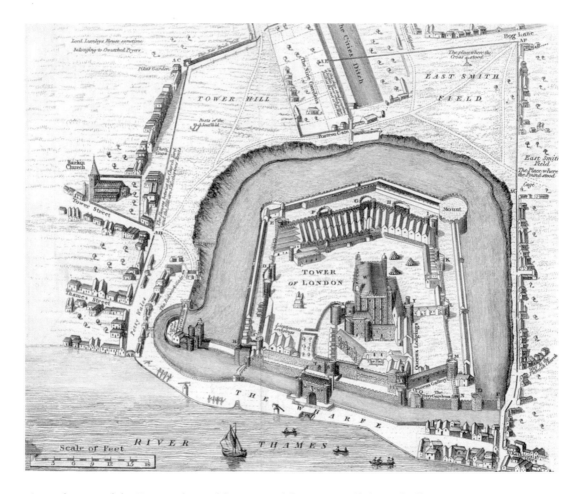

An early map of the Tower of London, where both Admiral Penn and his son William were imprisoned for various offenses against the government. Tower Hill, where William Penn's parents first lived after their marriage, is shown here in the upper left.

his teens with strong religious feelings.

William's life was abruptly shaken out of its familiar course when a crisis occurred in Admiral Penn's career. The expedition that Cromwell had sent to the Caribbean failed to capture Hispaniola. The failure was not the fault of Admiral Penn, who commanded the ships and sailors; the expedition's soldiers, commanded by General Robert Venables, had been beaten back by heat, hunger, and disease as much as by the Spanish garrison. Unwilling to return to England empty-handed, Admiral Penn took the fleet to Jamaica, another Spanish-occupied island in the Caribbean, and captured it. Cromwell was furious. The lord protector was a tyrant who expected his orders to be followed to the letter, and even though Jamaica was a richer prize than Hispaniola, he complained that the expedition's leaders had not done what he had told them to do. Upon their return to London, Venables and Penn were thrown into the Tower of London. The official reason for their imprisonment was that they had come home without orders to do so, but there were rumors that Penn had secretly offered to turn the whole fleet over to Charles II.

Once again, nothing could be proved against Admiral Penn, and he was released from the Tower after only five weeks. But he was now tainted by the suspicion of Royalist sympathies. The navy stripped him of his command and forced him to retire. Penn's downfall was both humiliating and terrifying for young William, who took great pride in his father's rank and heroism. It was an early lesson in the fickleness of fame and fortune—a lesson that William was to learn again, when he, too, was unjustly imprisoned.

After his release from the Tower, William's father decided to move his family to his Irish estate, hoping that he could support the household on the rents paid by his tenant farmers. In 1656 William was taken out of school, and the Penns crossed the Irish Sea to settle at Macroom.

Macroom Castle was a large, square, three-storied tower of gray stone; outside the castle walls was a village where the tenant farmers lived. William's family spent four years at Macroom. The house was usually full of friends and family members, including William's cousin, Uncle George's son, who was also named William. The admiral was both angry and melancholy about his fall from grace, and to cheer himself up he surrounded himself with relatives and seafaring cronies. Sadly, he also began drinking heavily. His son, meanwhile, pursued his studies at home, perhaps with the help of a tutor, and for recreation he and his cousin rambled through the nearby moors and fields.

Young William may have met some Quakers during this

time, either at Macroom or in the city of Cork, 26 miles away, where a small meeting, or congregation, of Friends had been established. Nearly 40 years later, Penn told a story about the visit of a well-known Quaker to Macroom Castle. He said that his father had heard of a man named Thomas Loe who had converted many people in Cork to Quakerism. The admiral broadmindedly invited Loe to visit Macroom, where Loe delivered a speech on the Inner Light—the Quaker belief that God resides in every man's and woman's soul and that every person can commune directly with God. This moving speech brought tears to the eyes of all listeners, from the crusty admiral to Anthony, the family's black slave.

Some scholars have suggested that perhaps Loe never really visited Macroom. They point out that throughout his life, Admiral Penn gave no evidence of being interested in religion, nor of being tolerant of Nonconformist sects. And no record exists of the visit except in William Penn's much later reference, written at a time when he may have been confused about the past. If the visit did occur, Loe's speech may have laid the groundwork for William's own conversion to Quakerism some years later.

After the Penns had been at Macroom for four years, events in the Commonwealth took a new direction. Oliver Cromwell died in 1658. His son, Richard, who succeeded him as lord protector, proved so weak and ineffective that he was nicknamed "Tumbledown Dick." Soon the country was in chaos. Cromwell's iron dictatorship had turned many against the Puritans, and now people across the country were beginning to call for the end of the Commonwealth and a return to the monarchy. Scores of plots arose to restore Charles II to the English throne. No one knows for certain what part, if any, Admiral Penn played in these conspiracies, but he is known to have been in contact with Royalist supporters. Early in 1660 he moved back to London. When a new parliament was formed, Admiral Penn was elected to it, along with many other

Royalists. In April the new parliament voted to invite
Charles II to return, and Admiral Penn—once more in the
thick of public affairs after four years of bitter isolation in
Ireland—was a member of the delegation that was sent to
the Netherlands to bring back the king.

The Protestant seminary at Saumur, France, where William Penn studied under Moïse Amyraut from 1662 to 1664. Amyraut's views on the importance of individual conscience in discerning divine truth greatly influenced Penn's own religious beliefs.

3

THE
YOUNG SEEKER

KING CHARLES II returned to England in grand style. The ship that carried him, christened the *Naseby* after a battle that Cromwell had won, was immediately rechristened the *Royal Charles* as the king stepped aboard. Once on the ship, Charles summoned Admiral Penn and dubbed him Sir William Penn, knight of the realm. Most historians believe that Penn must have given substantial aid to the Royalist cause to be rewarded in this way.

The monarch's triumphant return marked an upswing in the fortunes of the Penns. The Royalist who had owned Macroom before the Penns received it demanded its return from the king. In exchange, Charles gave Sir William an even larger Irish estate called Shanagarry, also near Cork. Furthermore, Sir William was appointed to a high-paying job as commissioner of the Royal Navy. He settled his family in a large new house in a section of Tower Hill where many naval officers and administrators lived. The Penns' neighbor was Samuel Pepys (pronounced "Peeps"), secretary of the navy's supply department, who kept a long and detailed diary describing the people and events of his time. Pepys's

Much of what we know about the young William Penn and his parents appears in the diary of the English politician Samuel Pepys. Although never intended for the public eye, Pepys's diary has become a classic in English literature.

diary, one of the most colorful sources of information about 17th-century London, contains many references to the Penn family. Pepys disliked all the Penns. He claimed that Margaret Penn was fat and dowdy and that her cooking "stank like the Devil." He thought young William was a conceited little prig. And he once wrote of Sir William, "I hate him with all my heart." Yet, like many bureaucrats, Pepys was skilled at hiding his true feelings and making himself agreeable to those in power. "Out of great and necessary discretion," as he described it, he passed himself off for years as a friend of the Penns.

Sir William and Lady Margaret embarked on a period of high living, with frequent riotous parties at which everyone drank heartily and engaged in crude practical jokes. Young William held himself aloof from these festivities, preferring to read in his attic bedroom. In the fall of 1660 he set off for Oxford, a university town north of London, for the next stage in his education. He was 16 years old, and his father had decided that he needed to acquire some polish and make friends among the well-born, newly restored Royalists.

Sir William enrolled his son in Christ Church, one of the most aristocratic colleges in Oxford. Penn was not an ordinary student. He held the rank of gentleman scholar, which meant that he was not really expected to work hard or to take his education seriously; he was one of 20 young men from noble or influential families who had special privileges and were thought to add prestige to the college. But William Penn was quite unlike the other gentlemen scholars of his time. His earnestness and his failure to do what was expected of him would enrage Sir William—and not for the last time. Penn's stay at Oxford marked the beginning of a long period of friction between the serious, idealistic young Penn and his conventional, ambitious, fierce-tempered father. In his own quiet way, William Penn was becoming a rebel.

Penn arrived at Oxford just as England was entering a period known as the Restoration because the Stuart dynasty, the royal family to which Charles I and Charles II belonged, had been restored to the throne. The Restoration was a free-spirited, pleasure-loving time, during which people reacted with glee to the lifting of Puritan restrictions. Theaters opened, and playwrights such as William Congreve produced witty comedies about romance and seduction. Poetry, music, and dancing, which had been outlawed by the dour Puritans, flourished during the Restoration. The Puritans had dressed in drab clothing, but during the 1660s, men and women alike wore fur capes, silk stockings, and clothing of bright blue and green satins and velvets decorated with ruffles, ribbons, and bows. The new freedom of the Restoration caused some people to go a bit wild; many wealthy young men thought of little but drinking, chasing women, brawling, and fighting duels. The king himself set a notorious example with many scandalous love affairs.

Penn did not really have the Restoration spirit. He had friends among his highborn, frivolous fellow students, but he was not satisfied by their pastimes. As a lonely, studious child reading his Bible, he had developed a deep spirituality that remained with him and grew even stronger once he entered the busy, worldly life of the university. Penn was searching for a sense of purpose or significance in his life, for enlightenment, and he privately felt that Oxford was "a signal place for idleness, loose living, profaneness, prodigality, and gross ignorance," filled with "hellish darkness and debauchery."

Penn had hoped that college would bring him into contact with other minds like his own—minds that had been formed by wide reading and that were eager to study and debate weighty questions of religion, philosophy, and politics. Although he did not find such intellectual companions among the jolly Cavaliers, he did meet a few kindred spirits at Oxford. The foremost of these was Dr. John Owen, a Puritan religious scholar who had been vice-chancellor of the university. When the Stuarts were restored, the Puritans fell into disfavor and the more traditional element within the Anglican Church returned to power. Owen was dismissed from his university post, but he continued to live just outside of Oxford, and he welcomed visits from students who wanted to discuss religion in an atmosphere of open-minded tolerance.

Owen encouraged his young followers to question the authority of the established church. An unusually free-thinking man for his time, he felt that the university should be a place for fair and unprejudiced debate, where students could examine new ideas—including the ideas of the Quakers and other Nonconformist religious groups who were generally scorned by both mainstream Anglicans and strict Puritans. William Penn became acquainted with Owen and began visiting his house on Sundays with a few like-minded young men. Owen greatly influenced Penn. Through his friendship with the older man, Penn learned to organize his thoughts and express his opinions—and also to respect free inquiry. John Owen did more than anyone else to help shape William Penn the writer and crusader for liberty.

In April 1661 Penn made his first visit home to London, covering 57 miles by stagecoach in one and a half days. A grand public celebration was planned to celebrate the coronation of Charles II, and Sir William wanted his son by his side. The Penns and the Pepyses went together to a rented room overlooking the route that the king and his procession would follow. The pageant was lavish. "So glorious was the show with gold and silver," wrote Pepys,

Christ Church in Oxford, England, where William Penn attended college as a "gentleman scholar." Here Penn met Dr. John Owen, perhaps the most important figure in his intellectual life.

"that we were not able to look at it, our eyes being so much overcome." Sir William swelled with pride when both King Charles and his brother, James, the duke of York, waved to him in greeting.

Penn started his second year at Oxford in the fall of 1662, and soon afterward Sir William began to worry about his son. He learned from the college authorities that William, along with several other young men, had stopped attending the chapel services that all students were required to attend. Instead, Penn and his friends were holding their own services at Dr. Owen's home. The authorities had warned the boys to stop visiting Owen, who was con-

Although Admiral Penn was not openly a Royalist, his fortunes improved when Charles II, shown here in a 17th-century engraving, was restored to the British throne. The Penns were granted an Irish estate called Shanagarry and Sir William received a prestigious and lucrative commission in the Royal Navy.

sidered a bad influence on their discipline and values, but the boys continued to call on their mentor. This defiant behavior puzzled and angered Sir William. He had intended for Penn to have all the social advantages of a fashionable education, and now the boy was demonstrating contempt for the way things were done. In January 1662 Sir William called Penn to London for a confrontation.

The meeting between father and son was awkward. Sir William was a domineering man of definite opinions, not likely to show much patience for anyone who disagreed with or defied him. And although most young people at times simmer with rebellion against their parents, Penn was becoming something more than an ordinary rebellious teenager. He was turning into a young man of independent mind who insisted on thinking for himself. Sir William thought this was a dangerous trend and gruffly ordered his son not to do anything that would make him stand out from the crowd. The admiral also began to think about transferring Penn from Oxford to Cambridge, another university, where the boy would be out of Owen's circle.

Before he returned to Oxford, Penn spent an afternoon alone roaming through London. At the docks he saw a ship being loaded for its voyage to the American colony, and he had what he later described as an "opening of joy," a moment of religious insight when he realized that in the New World across the ocean, people could live and think in new and freer ways. Years later, he would test this idea by founding Pennsylvania.

Penn went back to Oxford, but he did not stay long. He was appalled by the false religion of many of the teachers and students, who piously attended chapel every day and then went home to commit as many sins as they could. He felt that it was hypocritical to profess to be a Christian but not live like one. So he continued to follow his conscience, ignoring the university chapel services and meeting with Dr. Owen to pray and discuss religion. Then, in March, he went home to London and announced that he had been expelled from Oxford.

Historians are puzzled by Penn's description of his expulsion. The records of Christ Church list every one of the students expelled over the generations, but Penn's name is not among them. Penn later said that he had been "banished" from Oxford for writing a book that criticized the established church. No such book or record of its existence has ever been found. Today, most scholars agree that when Penn described his departure from Oxford—years after it happened—he had either knowingly exaggerated or had made a mistake. More likely, Penn probably just withdrew from the college in disgust and frustration.

It must have been difficult for Penn to tell his father that he was not going back to school. Sir William did not receive the news gracefully. According to Penn's own account, Sir William beat him and turned him out of the house. Penn was able to come home a few hours later, but the gossipy Pepys noted in his diary that the boy looked quite unwell and that father and son appeared to be on bad terms with one another.

Hoping that a change of scene would snap the boy out of his odd religious mood, Sir William sent Penn to France. In July 1662, traveling with the earl of Crawford and several other young noblemen, Penn crossed the English Channel and made his way to Paris.

The admiral's plan almost worked. Europe was exciting, and Penn was caught up in the sights and sounds of a new environment. For a few months he lived the typical life of a wealthy Englishman in Paris: having stylish new clothes made by the best tailors, seeing sights such as the cathedral of Notre Dame, and copying the elaborate manners of the members of the French court. Among other things, he learned about a new fad in France: the napkin. (One brand-new etiquette manual said that every gentleman should know 27 ways to fold a napkin.) Once he had mastered court etiquette, Penn was presented to King Louis XIV—a sign of tremendous social success. Soon, however, a shocking incident changed the course of his life and drove him back to the spiritual quest he had begun at Oxford.

Late one night, as Penn was returning through the dark Paris streets to his lodgings, a harsh voice rang out. A man suddenly ordered Penn to defend himself. The belligerent stranger said that he had just walked past and had taken off his hat to Penn. By the rules of etiquette Penn should have taken off his own hat in return. This custom, called "hat honor," was a courtesy practiced among gentlemen, and the stranger was insulted that Penn had not observed it. He challenged Penn to a sword fight. In vain, Penn explained that in the shadowy street he had not even seen the man pass and that he meant no discourtesy. The man drew his sword. There was a brief clash of arms and Penn, through luck or skill, disarmed his opponent. Now the advantage lay with Penn. He had been challenged, and he had won. He would be within his rights, as they were understood by gentlemen of the time, if he ran his opponent through the heart. Instead, Penn picked up the man's fallen sword, handed it to him with a bow, and walked on.

The encounter lasted only a few minutes, yet it lingered in Penn's thoughts for a long time, troubling him. What kind of "honor" caused men to fight to the death over the raising of a hat? "I ask any man of understanding or conscience if the whole round of ceremony was worth the life of a man," Penn wrote. He was perplexed and full of questions, and he decided to leave Paris and look for the answers. His search took him to Saumur, a small Protestant seminary, or religious college, on the Loire River in central France. One of the leading professors at Saumur was Moïse Amyraut, a lawyer turned teacher, who claimed that any man or woman could understand God's laws by studying his or her own heart. Amyraut's beliefs, in fact, were close to those of the Friends. It is not known how Penn happened to come to Saumur; perhaps his friend John Owen had advised him to study with Amyraut.

In any event, Penn spent a year or more at Saumur. Although he was not formally enrolled in the seminary, he lived in Amyraut's house and followed a course of reading laid out for him by the liberal professor. In long discussions about the Bible, historical events, and current political affairs, Penn sharpened his insights and his debating skills. He also devoted considerable time to prayer and quiet meditation. He felt himself moving further and further away from the conventional doctrines of the Church of England, but he did not yet identify with any other faith. He knew only that he was searching for a form of worship that placed more value on individual conscience than on priestly hierarchy.

Amyraut died in 1664, and Penn left Saumur. Back in

The Parliamentarian Algernon Sidney remained exiled from England from 1659 until long after Charles II was restored to the throne. A fierce advocate of nonconformists, Sidney's views on government by the people intrigued the young Penn.

Paris he met a former Oxford classmate, Robert Spencer, the future earl of Sunderland. Spencer proposed that they travel together to Italy, and Penn eagerly agreed. He had a wonderful time on the trip, delighting in the mild, almost tropical warmth of southern France and the grandeur of the Alps. But when the two men reached the city of Turin in northern Italy, Penn found a message from Sir William. England and the Netherlands were about to go to war, said Sir William, and Penn was to come home at once while he could still do so.

On his way home, Penn met Algernon Sidney, an Englishman living in exile in Europe. Sidney believed that England should be a republic and that ordinary people should choose their leaders. Such republicanism was dangerously radical at the time, and Charles II would not allow Sidney to spread his ideas in England. But Penn was stimulated by his conversations with the political theorist. Along with his meditations on religion and conscience, Penn now began to consider whether government ought to be by the free consent of the governed, rather than by force or tradition.

In August 1664 Penn arrived in London after an absence of two years. Sir William and Lady Margaret were pleased to see their son clad in bright, fashionable clothes, using graceful French manners, and speaking knowledgeably of King Louis and other European notables. But Samuel Pepys confided sourly in his diary that Penn had "a great deale, if not too much, of the vanity of the French." He added, "I fear all profit he has made in his travels will signify little."

By now Penn was nearly 20 years old. We do not know for certain what he looked like. None of the few portraits that exist was painted from life; they are all copies of originals that are now lost. But from various descriptions, we do know that Penn was considered tall and that he became stout as he grew older. His hair was probably light brown and his eyes were large and dark. He wore his hair in long locks, but it was thin, possibly as a result of his childhood bout with smallpox. On the whole, he was a presentable young man, and Sir William hoped that he would reach great heights at court. The admiral decided that the next step in Penn's education should be the study of law. He did not really expect his son to become a lawyer, but the London law colleges, called the Inns of Court, were like Oxford—a place for a young man to rub elbows with other sons of the rich and powerful. In February 1665, therefore, Penn was enrolled in Lincoln's Inn, an ancient and prestigious law school.

But Penn's time at Lincoln's Inn was short. Before the end of his first semester, he was called away by his father. England and the Netherlands were once again at war, and Admiral Penn was going to sail against the Dutch fleet as he had done in the heroic days of 1653. This time, however, William was no longer a small boy waiting anxiously at home to hear the outcome of the battle. This time, William Penn was going to battle too.

This image of a youthful William Penn clad in armor is one of many copies of an original painting commissioned by Penn himself. Penn had decided to become a soldier shortly before he attended his first Quaker meeting.

4

IRELAND AND
THE QUAKERS

IRONICALLY, THE MAN who later became a pacifist enjoyed his first experience of war. Penn was neither a soldier nor a sailor, and he was not an officer; he was a volunteer aide to his father. In those days, many young gentlemen went to battle in this informal way in order to acquire martial glory. Sir William, who dreamed of a high-level court appointment for his son, wanted Penn to accompany him so that the young man could meet and make a good impression on James, the duke of York, who was lord high admiral of the English fleet. As the great captain commander, Sir William officially took orders from the duke, but in reality he commanded the fleet himself, for James lacked the experience to do so. Penn was part of Sir William's staff on the flagship *Royal Charles*, where he met James, the king's brother. The two remained on good terms for many years.

Penn liked life aboard ship and even showed signs of interest in a naval career. But he did not remain on the *Royal Charles* for long. After only a month or so, Sir William sent his son back to London to carry secret dispatches, or papers, to the king. Charles II received the

Penn met the Duke of York, who would later assume the crown as James II, while serving under his father in the Royal Navy. After James's conversion to Catholicism sometime between 1668 and 1671, Catholics and other nonconformists enjoyed unprecedented religious liberties.

dispatches in person and held a short conversation with Penn, during which he praised Sir William and asked about his welfare. This episode seems to have impressed Penn mightily. He felt a new admiration and affection for his father after seeing him in command of a fleet and respected by royalty.

But Penn did not return to the *Royal Charles*. Sir William had acccomplished his mission—introducing his son to the king and the duke of York—so he directed Penn to return to Lincoln's Inn and resume his studies. Penn dutifully wrote to Sir William: "As I never knew what a father was until I had wisdom to praise him, so can I safely say that now, of all times, your concerns are most dear to me. 'Tis hard meanwhile to lose both a father and a friend." The relationship between father and son, so often turbulent, had become closer and warmer.

As it happened, Penn was back at Lincoln's Inn for just a few weeks before a dire emergency closed the law school. London was in the grip of bubonic plague, a virulent epidemic of a disease that was also called the Black Death. The plague, transmitted by fleas that were carried from city to city by rats, had ravaged Europe several times in the past. In the 14th century it killed a quarter of the population of the continent, and in 1625 another outbreak claimed the lives of 40,000 Londoners. In 1665, just as the Dutch and English fleets were maneuvering for battle, the Black Death struck again. The Great Plague of London killed more than 100,000 people between the spring of 1665 and December of that year. At the height of the plague, 7,000 died weekly, and corpse-haulers trundled carts through the city, mournfully chanting, "Bring out your dead." Those who could do so fled the pestilent city for the countryside. London became a ghost town, occupied only by the poor, the dying, and the criminals who preyed upon them. The city would suffer a second devastating blow in September 1666, when it was swept by the Great Fire, the worst conflagration in London's history.

The fire destroyed four-fifths of the city.

One result of the plague and the fire was an increase in the activity of Nonconformist religious groups, many of whom preached that God was punishing the city for its sins. The Quakers did not promote this blood-and-thunder belief, but they were much in evidence during the disasters, for many of them remained in the city to nurse the sick and help the homeless. The plague also stirred Penn's thoughts about the impermanence of human life. He later wrote, "In the time of the Great Plague of London, the Lord gave me a deep sense of the Vanity of this World, of the Irreligiousness of the Religions in it."

Although the Penn family survived the plague, they faced other problems. The English fleet had defeated the Dutch in battle on June 3, but the English had unaccountably failed to follow up this victory by pursuing the fleeing Dutch vessels and wiping out the whole enemy fleet. The duke of York, who had not ordered pursuit, was officially to blame for this failure, but Sir William Penn stepped forward to take the blame, allowing people to think that he had advised the duke against pursuit. In this way, the king's brother was spared harsh criticism.

Sir William, however, received plenty of criticism. Old accusations of cowardice and drunkenness were revived, and once again Sir William's enemies whispered that he had pocketed money that should have been spent on supplies for his men. The Stuarts were privately grateful that Sir William had saved the duke from embarrassment, but they thought Sir William should withdraw from the public eye for a time. So the hot-tempered sea captain, who had begun to suffer from the painful disease of gout, returned home to London. The plans he had made to request an appointment to the navy staff for his son were postponed. Instead, he sent Penn to Ireland on business related to the Shanagarry estate.

Penn arrived in Ireland in January 1666. After finishing his duties at Shanagarry, he went to Dublin and fell in with a lively set of sophisticated young men who spent their time discussing art, flirting with the local belles, and gossiping about their acquaintances among the nobility. Recalling this period, Penn later admitted, "The glory of the world was with me, and I was ever ready to give myself to it." Penn not only experimented with novel social distractions, but also sought a second taste of military adventure.

When mutiny broke out among some English soldiers stationed in Ireland, Penn was among a number of gallant gentlemen who voluntarily joined forces to quell the revolt. The mutineers were quickly overcome, and Penn, excited by the victory, decided to become a soldier. Around this time he had a portrait of himself painted, in which he appears as a young, wavy-haired man with a gentle but somber expression, clad in dark armor. The original portrait has been lost, but three copies of it, made in the 18th century, survive. They are thought to be the closest we have to an accurate image of Penn.

Penn was offered the captaincy of a garrison in Ireland, but Sir William ordered him not to accept it. The admiral may have been pleased that his son was showing an interest in the manly art of soldiering, but he did not want Penn to be buried in an insignificant Irish command. "He shall dig potatoes first," the indignant Sir William declared. He thought a captaincy was not good enough for his son, for whom he envisioned a glorious career at court. The relationship between father and son again grew strained, with Penn chafing against his father's strict control. Before long, however, events turned Penn away both from the army and the court.

He was in Cork one day when he happened to chat with a shopkeeper there—some accounts say that he recognized her from his time at Macroom years before. She was a Quaker, many of whom made their livings as owners of shops and small businesses. Customers liked dealing with them because, unlike most merchants, the Quakers did not haggle or bargain over prices. Instead, they set a fixed price for their goods and charged everyone the same amount, because they believed it was important to practice fairness and equality in everyday matters.

According to Penn's account of this encounter, he mentioned that he had once heard a Quaker named Thomas Loe speak, and he added that he would gladly travel a hundred miles to hear him again. No need to go so far, the woman replied. Loe was in Cork to attend a Quaker meeting. Penn was welcome to come and hear him there, if he wished. Penn promised he would do so.

Whether or not he had really heard Loe at Macroom, Penn was apparently curious about the Quakers. He kept his promise and attended the meeting, where Loe spoke eloquently on the idea that "there is a faith which overcomes the world and a faith which is overcome by the world." Penn was deeply impressed by a faith that remained true to its inner convictions, regardless of the rules and limitations placed upon it by bishops and kings. He later said of his experience, "the Lord visited me with a certain sound and testimony of his Eternal word." The Friends used the word "convincement" to describe Penn's experience: the moment when someone is suddenly filled with a profound inner certainty of God's presence. In Quaker terms, Penn was convinced that day in Cork. At last he had found what he had been searching for ever since his childhood, when he pored over his Bible and tried to understand God's will. He declared that he intended to join the Friends.

This was a momentous decision, even a dangerous one. The Friends were subject to much persecution, and by associating with them Penn risked similar treatment. As he spent more time with his new Quaker friends, Penn learned that they had had trouble with government authorities from the start.

Quakerism was an outgrowth of a mass religious movement of the 17th century during which people

The only known likeness of George Fox, the founder of the sect originally known as "Children of Light." Today, members of the Religious Society of Friends are commonly called Quakers.

throughout Europe pulled away from their established churches. In England, Puritanism gained strength and scores of entirely new sects sprang up. Among these were the Ranters, the Diggers, the Levelers, the Baptists, the Seekers, the Muggletonians, the Fifth Monarchists, and many more. Most of these Nonconformist or Dissenting groups preached a simplified form of Protestantism, stripped of tradition and priestly show. They emphasized the individual and the importance of seeking truth through one's own conscience. Some of these sects vanished almost as suddenly as they had appeared; others established their places in history.

One of those caught up in this religious ferment in 1643, a year before Penn was born, was a young man named George Fox. Dismayed by people who attended church regularly but still lived sinful, greedy lives, Fox wandered from sect to sect in search of a faith that would unite the spiritual and the worldly. Gradually, he began speaking about his own beliefs and won followers. By 1652 his followers, who called themselves the Children of Light or the Friends of Truth, had become a significant sect. Their chief principles were that God speaks directly to any heart that opens itself to hear (this was called the doctrine of the Inner Light), that formal churches and preachers are unnecessary, and that people should live as Jesus Christ did, reflecting in every action their inmost beliefs. The Friends stressed simplicity, fairness, and equality. Because they believed that no person is inherently better than any other, they refused to perform the customary hat honor and they also used the terms "thee" and "thou" instead of "you" when speaking to others (at that time "thee" and "thou" were used only to address servants, children, and social inferiors, while people of superior standing were addressed as "you"). These egalitarian practices irked many wellborn people, and the Friends' rejection of the established religion was a thorn in the side of both the state and the church. The Quakers often got into

trouble because they refused to pay tithes, or church taxes, to the Anglican Church and also because they refused to take oaths—that is, to swear to something on God's name.

The term "Quaker" came into use early in the movement. Some people said that the Friends were called Quakers because they trembled, or quaked, with intense feeling during their meetings. Fox himself said that the name was coined in 1650 by a justice of the peace when Fox warned the official to "tremble at the Word of the Lord." Whatever its origin, the name was soon adopted, and before long it was no longer considered an insult; many Quakers, including William Penn, used it to refer to themselves. But they continued to call themselves Friends, and they addressed one another as "Friend Fox," "Friend Penn," and so on. Today the worldwide community of Quakers is

The Friends met with persecution not only from the Church of England, but also in New England by the Puritans, as shown in this engraving. Ironically, the Puritans themselves traveled across the sea to North America in search of religious freedom.

A follower of George Fox is publicly flogged in the streets of England.

called the Society of Friends, a name that came into use in the late 18th century.

The Quakers were misunderstood, feared, and hated by many people. Some people disliked the Quakers simply because they were different—they dressed plainly, spoke modestly, and seemed to live outside of conventional society. Although their beliefs were somewhat similar to those of the Puritans, the Quakers were persecuted as viciously by intolerant Puritans as they were by traditional Anglicans. Indeed, four Quakers were hanged in Boston by the Puritans—who had themselves fled to Massachusetts to find religious freedom. Both the Commonwealth and the Restoration periods were difficult for the Quakers as well as for other Nonconformists. Laws were passed forbidding free speech and assemblies for such groups. One prominent Quaker, James Naylor, was convicted of blasphemy in 1656 for preaching his religious views; his punishment was to have a hole burned through his tongue with a red-hot poker. Between 1650 and 1689, thousands of Quakers were thrown into prison and as many as 450 of them died there. Following one's conscience against the rest of the world is always difficult, but in the 17th century it was heroic.

Penn's enthusiasm was unquenched by the fear of persecution. He was young and vigorous, ready—and even eager—to overcome obstacles for his newfound faith. The teachings of John Owen and Moïse Amyraut had led him to believe that everyone should be free to think, pray, and worship in his or her own way.

Penn began attending Quaker meetings in Cork and other communities in eastern Ireland. The meetings were held in secret to avoid harassment or arrest. But these precautions failed on September 3, 1667, when the rowdy soldier interrupted the Friends meeting in Cork, leading to Penn's arrest—and to his declaration that he was a Quaker. Penn's letter to the powerful earl of Orrery brought the release of all the Quakers from the Cork jail, but another hurdle lay ahead: Penn had to face his father.

Orrery wrote to Sir William, telling him what his son had been up to in Ireland. The admiral was furious that Penn had gone so far as to identify himself with an outlaw sect. He wrote the following letter from the Navy Office on October 12, 1667. "Son William," it began,

I have writ several letters to you since I received any from you. By this I charge you strictly and command that you come to me with all possible speed. In expectation of your compliance, I remain, Your affectionate father, W. Penn.

Penn did not respond at once, claiming that he still had business to attend to at Shanagarry. On October 22 the impatient admiral wrote again:

I hope this will find you in health. The cause of this writing is to charge you to repair to me with all possible speed, presently after your receipt of it, and not make any stay there, or any other place on the road, until it pleases God you see me (unless for necessary rest and refreshment). Your affectionate father, W. Penn.

In other words, Penn was to drop everything and come home at once, pausing only to sleep and eat. But Penn did not depart for London until December, and then he did not go alone. One of his new acquaintances, a Quaker named Josiah Coale, came with him—a circumstance that was not likely to delight Sir William.

Indeed, the gout-ridden admiral, already facing a formal impeachment on charges of embezzling naval funds, was in no mood to humor his son's religious fancies. One dramatic version of their meeting says that Penn threatened to throw himself out of a window rather than renounce his Quakerism, but this colorful tale is based only on legends and there is no reliable account of it. What is known, however, is that Sir William ordered Penn to give up his Quaker nonsense, that Penn refused, and that the admiral reacted with anger and deep disappointment. He must have felt that the boy was deliberately throwing away the fine future for which the admiral had worked so hard to prepare him. But to Penn, the matter was one of conscience and integrity. Having found his faith, he would not be shaken.

Not only did Penn continue to call himself a Quaker,

but he also attended meetings of Friends in and around London. Already he was defining a role for himself among the Friends. Better educated—and certainly better connected—than most of them, he would become their foremost spokesperson. George Fox, Thomas Loe, and others were brilliant speakers, but the movement lacked a writer who could explain and defend Quakerism and record its history and development for future members. Penn filled that role. And with his contacts in high places and his smattering of legal knowledge, he would leap to the defense of Quakers who were arrested or persecuted.

During the first few months of 1668, relations between Penn and his father were strained almost to the breaking point. Penn was frequently away from home on Quaker business. The charges against the admiral were dropped and he returned to work at the Navy Office. But he was unable to celebrate; he was worried about his son. Then, Penn was arrested again. This time the magistrate refused to imprison him, but he told Sir William to give his son a warning. Enraged at this public humiliation, Sir William ordered Penn to move out of the house, declaring that he would leave his estate "to them that pleased him better." It seemed that the rift between these two stubborn souls had finally widened beyond all hope of mending.

Imprisoned several times for his religious and political beliefs, Penn used the time to write a number of important treatises on individual freedom, including his explication of Sandy Foundations Shaken, *which he titled* Innocency with Her Open Face *(1669), and* The Great Case of Liberty of Conscience *(1671), a defense of toleration.*

5

TRIALS

PENN THREW HIMSELF into his new life as a Quaker. Although he remained in touch with his family, he now traveled and lived with other Quakers. In July 1668 he toured the country with Coale and Loe, urging others to join the Quakers. Penn's strength was in attacking vanity and the false pleasures of worldly goods. Even though he still wore better clothes than his fellow Quakers and had not removed the fancy plume from his hat, he was now considerably more drab in appearance than most gentlemen of the period. In his talks, he tore into those who prided themselves on their lavish dress, saying, "How many pieces of ribbon, feathers, lace bands and the like had Adam and Eve in Paradise or out of it?" He demanded to know whether the Virgin Mary had used face powder or worn "false locks of strange colours." On this tour he also met George Fox, with whom he would later become friends. Much of what we know about Fox's character and actions comes from Penn's writings.

The tour led the traveling Quakers though Buckinghamshire, where they called on Penn's childhood acquaintance, Gulielma Springett.

Penn wrote the most important of his works, No Cross, No Crown, *while imprisoned in the Tower of London. The treatise defends Quaker doctrines and practices, and criticizes the un-Christian behavior of England's clergy.*

135

NO
Crofs, no Crovvn :
Or feveral Sober
REASONS
Againft
Hat-Honour, *Titular-Refpeels,* **You** to a fingle Perfon, with the *Apparel* and *Recreations* of the Times :

Being inconfiftant with Scripture, Reafon, and the Practice, as well of the beft Heathens, as the holy Men and Women of all Generations; and confequently fantaftick, impertinent and finfull.

With Sixty Eight Teftimonies of the moft famous Perfons, of both former and latter Ages for further confirmation.

In Defence of the poor defpifed *Quakers,* againft the Practice and Objections of their Adverfaries.

By W. Penn *j.*
An humble Difciple, and patient Bearer of the Crofs of Jefus.

But Mordecai *bowed not,* Efth. 3. 2. Adam *where art thou?* Gen. 3. 9. *In like manner the women adorn themfelves in modeft Apparal, not with brodered hair, &c.* 1 Tim. 2. 9. *Thy Law is my Meditation all the day;* Pfal. 119. 97.

Printed in the Year, 1669.

Like her stepbrother, Isaac Penington, she had become a Quaker. After this visit, Penn and Gulielma began corresponding. Penn addressed her as Guli and also signed his letters Guli, a shortened form of Gulielmus, which is Latin for William.

Penn's role as a spokesman for the Friends resulted in his imprisonment in the Tower of London in late 1668. A Presbyterian minister named Thomas Vincent had been attacking the Quakers in violently offensive speeches, and Penn—who had matured as a debater under the tutelage of

Owen and Amyraut—challenged Vincent to a public debate at which both sides could present their arguments. Vincent agreed, but he insisted that the debate be held in his own chapel. When Penn and his fellow Quakers arrived, they found the building filled with Vincent's noisy supporters. Vincent spoke first, and he spoke for hours— one source says he prayed aloud until after midnight. As soon as he finished, he and his followers trooped out, leaving Penn no chance to respond.

Vincent then published a pamphlet called *The Foundations of God Standeth*, in which he continued his attack on the Friends. Stung to anger, Penn wrote a reply called *Sandy Foundations Shaken*. Unfortunately, it was hastily written and included some language that was interpreted as an attack on the established church and the state, although such things were far from Penn's intention. Some highly placed persons in the Church of England declared that *Sandy Foundations Shaken* was blasphemous—that is, that it undermined official church doctrine. Because the king of England was also the formal head of the Church of England, an attack on the Church was also considered an attack on the state, and blasphemy could also be interpreted as treason. Penn was thrown into the Tower under suspicion of both.

At first he was held in solitary confinement in a cold, dismal cell. After a week or so, he received a message from the archbishop of London stating that unless he admitted to blasphemy and apologized for it, he would remain in prison until he died. Penn replied that he had committed neither blasphemy nor treason and would not apologize, for he had done nothing wrong. "My prison shall be my grave before I will budge a jot, for I owe my conscience to no mortal man," he is said to have responded.

A week or so later, Penn was moved to better quarters and his servant, Francis Cooke, was permitted to bring him fresh clothing. The archbishop then sent Edward Stillingfleet, the bishop of London, to reason with Penn.

But the plan backfired when Penn and Stillingfleet became friends. Although neither could fully accept the other's views, they liked and respected one another, and their debates were probably the most pleasant feature of Penn's jail term.

Penn was also able to write letters to Guli and other friends and to work on more religious pamphlets. The most important of these was a treatise called *No Cross, No Crown*, in which Penn called for a return to the simplicity and purity of early Christianity, before faith became cluttered up with ritual and pomp. Over the years, Penn revised and expanded *No Cross, No Crown* several times, and it became one of his most influential and enduring works.

Meanwhile, efforts were under way to release Penn from prison. Sir William wrote to the king's council pleading for his son's release and lamenting that Penn's Quakerism had been "a great affliction." (Unknown to Penn, Sir William had softened somewhat toward his wayward son and had drawn up a new will that left him the bulk of the Penn estate.) At the same time, Penn himself moved on two fronts. First, he petitioned the king for release, saying that he had been imprisoned without a fair trial, which was every Englishman's right. Second, with Stillingfleet's help, he wrote a pamphlet called *Innocency with Its Open Face*, in which he explained that *Sandy Foundations Shaken* had been aimed not at the Church of England but only at Vincent—a Dissenter who was highly critical of the established church.

Penn's release on July 28, 1669, was probably the result of all these factors. He was set free after seven and one-half months in the Tower. In the eyes of the Quakers, he was now a hero and martyr who had proved his commitment to their cause. But to many outside the Quaker movement, controversy and imprisonment had tainted Penn. There were even rumors that he was a Catholic spy—a serious accusation at a time when Protestant England was rabidly hostile toward Catholic nations such as France and

Spain and many Englishmen feared Catholic plots to take over their country.

Although the Stuarts had Catholic sympathies (the duke of York was a practicing Catholic), they wanted to allay the fears of the Protestant Parliament, so they enacted strict anti-Catholic laws and allowed Catholics to be cruelly persecuted. Somehow the notion entered the public mind that Penn might be mixed up with the Catholics. People hinted that he refused to raise his hat because he had the shaven head of a Catholic priest. Or perhaps the "Saumur" where he claimed to have studied was really St. Omer, a well-known Catholic seminary. These rumors were utterly false and ridiculous, but Sir William nevertheless thought it best to keep Penn out of the mainstream of London society for a time, so he sent Penn back to Shanagarry. Intending to devote all his time to writing and missionary work, Penn hired a Quaker colleague named Philip Ford to serve as the steward, or manager, of the estate. He would regret this decision years later.

On their way to Ireland, Penn and Ford stopped to visit Guli Springett; some accounts say that Penn and Guli became engaged during this visit. Then the two men crossed the Irish Sea, reaching Cork in October 1669. Penn found that many Quakers had been imprisoned in Ireland, and through persistent visits to high-ranking authorities—who could not turn him away for fear of offending Sir William—Penn was able to get them released. He returned to England in June 1670, leaving Ford in charge at Shanagarry.

Later that summer Penn and other Quaker leaders decided on a bold plan to prove that Quaker meetings were not political conspiracies and should be legalized. Penn announced that he and William Mead, another prominent Quaker, would hold a public religious meeting, in violation of strict new laws. When police constables barred the doors of the meetinghouse, Penn and Mead convened their meeting in the street. The constables began to arrest them

Gulielma Springett married her childhood friend William Penn in 1672. The Penns had six children, including sons Springett and William and daughter Letitia as well as three others who died in infancy. Guli Penn died in 1694.

on charges of preaching in a public thoroughfare. A scuffle broke out in the crowd, and the charge was changed to the much more serious one of inciting a riot. Penn and Mead were brought to trial before Sir Samuel Starling, the lord mayor of London, on September 3, 1670.

Starling was not an impartial justice. He ordered the court bailiffs to snatch Penn's and Mead's hats, then fined the two men for failing to remove their headgear in court. He made disparaging remarks about Penn's father, calling him "Sir William who starved the sailors." He would not let Penn, who was acting as lawyer for Mead and himself, cross-examine any of the witnesses. But Starling's hostility toward the two Quakers backfired. Such obvious and heavy-handed malice offended the jury and tilted the jurors in favor of the defendants. When the verdict was delivered, Mead was found innocent, and Penn was found guilty only of preaching in the street.

The verdict provoked an uproar. Sir Samuel angrily ordered the jurors to reconsider. They did so, but delivered the same verdict. Then Sir Samuel declared that he would hold them without food and drink until they found both defendants guilty of inciting a riot.

Penn's trial was already important to his fellow Quakers. Now it took on a grave importance for all the people of England. The very heart of England's judicial system was the concept of trial by jury, and suddenly the freedom of jurors to deliver a verdict without bullying or fear of reprisals was threatened. The jury's foreman, Edward Bushell, clearly saw the significance of the occasion. He fortified the resolve of the other jurors, and although the lord mayor held them prisoner for two days without food or access to toilets, they did not waver. Instead, when Sir Samuel called them back into court, expecting an obedient verdict of "guilty on all counts," the jurors announced that they now found *both* defendants innocent on all counts. The vindictive mayor fined each juror for contempt of court. They all refused to pay. So Sir Samuel ordered them

all to Newgate Prison—the dirty, crowded, disease-infest-ed prison of debtors and common criminals—and sent Penn and Mead to Newgate along with them.

Sir William was distressed to see his son in jail again, this time in a filthy commoners' prison. For a change, he agreed with Penn's principles, but he urged his son to pay his fines and get out of jail. The admiral was gravely ill and was afraid he would die without seeing his son again. Penn said that he could not give in and pay, so the admiral secretly paid for both Penn and Mead, and the two Quak-ers were released. Eight jurors also paid their fines, but Bushell and three others staunchly refused. They were released on bail two months later, and when they came to trial for contempt, the lord chief justice of England upheld their case. In effect, the outcome of the trial was a confir-

A typical Quaker meeting at Jordan Meeting House, near Chalfont St. Giles in Bucking-hamshire, England, where Guli Springett and William Penn worshiped. Serene gath-erings such as this were viewed as treasonous by the British government until James II assumed the throne.

mation of the jury's right to make an independent decision. Scholars of the law hail this case as a landmark in judicial history, and the real credit goes not to Penn or Mead but to Edward Bushell, the jury foreman, who would not save himself by letting the judge bend the law.

Penn left Newgate just in time for a final meeting with his father. The admiral still did not approve of the course Penn had chosen, but he loved his son and hoped to part from him on good terms. He died a week after Penn was released from prison. After his father's funeral, Penn wrote a pamphlet called *Truth Rescued from Impostors* defending Sir William against the rumors and suspicions that had haunted the elder man's career.

His long struggle with his father was over, and Penn had inherited a great deal of money. He was readier than ever to devote himself to full-time Quaker activity. His polished speeches and writings attracted many converts to the Friends. Among them were rich or highborn men and women who were willing to listen to Penn but who would have disregarded Fox or Loe, who were self-educated commoners. Before long, though, Penn was arrested again, and he was sentenced to six months in Newgate for refusing to swear an oath.

As before, Penn used the time in jail to write, producing an important work called *The Great Case of Liberty of Conscience*, which calls for both religious toleration and political rights. Its underlying principle is that people are basically reasonable beings who will naturally make the right decisions about worship and government; therefore they should be left free to worship as they please, and they should have a greater voice in the government.

Upon his release from Newgate in August 1671, Penn made a second trip to Europe. This time he headed not for the glittering festivities of Paris but to the Netherlands and Germany, where he met with members of other Nonconformist groups and tried to make converts for the Friends. (Fox and a few others had just sailed across the Atlantic to

America on a similar mission.) But Penn's trip was unsuccessful and he wanted to see Guli, so he returned to England in October. There he was asked to take on many of Fox's responsibilities for organizing the Friends and maintaining communication among meetings in different parts of the country.

Fox returned from America in 1673, but after a few months he was arrested and imprisoned under the provisions of a law called the Test Act, which required people to swear allegiance to the king. Constables and magistrates had taken to arresting Quakers on trivial charges and then, before dismissing them from court, asking them to swear the oath of loyalty. When they refused to use God's name to swear an oath, the Quakers were imprisoned for violating the Test Act. Fox remained in jail until 1675. During

Worminghurst Place in County Sussex, England. The Penns moved to this estate, which Guli inherited from the Springett family, in 1676.

Fox's imprisonment, Penn once again took on many of the tasks of Quaker leadership.

Penn also assumed more personal responsibilities. He married Guli Springett on April 4, 1672, and the couple settled in a town called Rickmansworth in southeast England and started a family. It was not uncommon in the 17th century for children to die in infancy; sadly, Penn's first three children met this fate. Penn's brother, Richard, also died around this time while visiting Penn. Fearing that Rickmansworth was unhealthful, Penn moved his family to an estate called Worminghurst in the open countryside of southern England just after his fourth child, a son named Springett, was born. This child survived the perils of infancy.

In 1677 Penn went back to Europe, this time accompanied by George Fox and other Friends. Traveling through the Netherlands, Belgium, and Germany, they met with religious leaders and made further missionary efforts to attract converts. Although few of those with whom they spoke actually joined, the Friends found that most people listened courteously and with interest—which must have been heartening, given the hostility the Friends often met at home.

Penn's family continued to grow in the following years. His daughter, Letitia, was born in 1678, and a son, William Jr., was born in the spring of 1680. By this time, Penn had become involved with an American venture. In 1674 he was asked to settle an argument between two English Quakers, John Fenwick and Edward Billinge, over the ownership of the southern part of the New Jersey colony, which they had bought from Lord Berkeley, the colony's proprietor (a proprietor held rights to a colony as a grant from the Crown). After reviewing the case, Penn decided that the property in question belonged to Billinge, who was deeply in debt. To raise money toward his debts, Billinge offered tracts of land to colonists willing to settle in the New World. Penn was one of the administrators of this colony. He and Billinge hoped to build a Quaker settlement there, and in 1677 they launched the settlement with 230 colonists. Penn also advised Billinge to draw up a charter of rights and freedoms for the colonists. Among other rights, this charter guaranteed freedom of religion and government by the people—foreshadowing some of the most important provisions of the United States Constitution.

Penn's involvement with the Billinge colony turned his thoughts toward America. He remembered the "opening of joy" he had felt years earlier when he watched a ship set sail for the New World. Although Quakers had been present in the American colonies almost since the beginning of their movement, they had encountered little toleration there. Now Penn began to think about starting an entirely new colony as a Quaker sanctuary. This was the genesis of Pennsylvania.

William Penn (right) receiving the Charter of Pennsylvania from Charles II in 1681.

6

THE HOLY
EXPERIMENT

PENN'S MUSINGS ABOUT a new colony in America took a great
leap forward in 1679. Until that year, Penn had optimistically believed
that reform was possible in England and that, given the chance, people
would create a more progressive, liberal government that allowed liberty of conscience and protected individual rights. When the political
philosopher Algernon Sidney came out of exile in 1679 to run for Parliament, Penn was overjoyed. He had admired Sidney since meeting
the older man in Europe years before. Sidney stood for everything
Penn hoped to see in a public figure.

But Sidney was soundly defeated, and Penn himself was forcibly
thrown out of the local polling place. He began to fear that parliamentary reform was impossible. Dejected, he concluded that all around
him immorality was flourishing while virtue was being persecuted.
From this time on, he believed that the New World offered the best
chance for reform.

With money at his command, a social status that gave him access to
most important people in the country, and a persuasive tongue and pen,

William Penn set out to win a grant of land from King Charles. He knew that Charles had owed a substantial sum of money to Sir William Penn and that the debt had not been repaid. Penn decided to approach the king by suggesting that a land grant would cancel the old debt to his father. Furthermore, he would point out that if a large number of Quakers settled in America, as Penn hoped they would, the Quakers would no longer be troublesome in England—for which the king should be grateful. Penn presented these arguments to carefully chosen allies in the royal court, and he accompanied them with discreet bribes—for he was not above using underhanded means to achieve such an important goal. One of his allies was the duke of York, who had always liked Penn. Another was Robert Spencer, the earl of Sunderland, with whom Penn had once toured France and Italy; Sunderland was now the king's secretary of state. He notified Penn when the king was in a favorable mood, and on June 1, 1680, Penn formally petitioned Charles for the large tract of land west of New Jersey, sandwiched between New York and Maryland. A richly wooded, fertile region, the land was cut by numerous rivers, with rolling hills in the east and rugged mountains in the north and west. Both Coale and Fox had seen the territory and had spoken of its beauties.

Years often passed before such petitions were granted or rejected, but in Penn's case the decision was made quickly, probably because Penn had generously bribed the right people. When it came to naming the new colony, however, disagreements arose. King Charles wanted to name it Pennsylvania, or "Penn's Woods," not after Penn himself but after his father the admiral, who had been instrumental in Charles's return to the throne. Penn did not like this idea. He was sure that his critics would think he had named the colony after himself and would accuse him of vanity. He asked Sir Leoline Jenkins, one of the king's counselors, to dissuade Charles from adopting this name. Unfortunately, Penn's suggestion, New Wales, named after

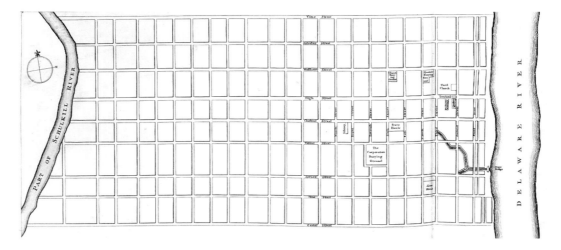

a hilly and wooded region in western England, offended Sir Leoline, who happened to be from Wales and was affronted at the comparison with a barbaric land inhabited by savages (the conventional English upper-class view of America and Native Americans). Leoline refused to raise the matter with the king, and the name Pennsylvania stood.

On March 14, 1681, King Charles II signed a document called the Charter of Pennsylvania. In return for a token annual rent—two beaver skins and one-fifth of any gold or silver that might be discovered on the land—Penn became the sole proprietor of the largest territory ever owned by a private British citizen. Only one individually owned colony in all of recorded history has ever been larger, and that was the Belgian Congo, which was the personal property of King Leopold II of Belgium during the late 19th century.

As proprietor, Penn's powers were sweeping. He could appoint officials and make laws. (Although in theory those laws had to be approved by officials in London, in practice the proprietors were rarely questioned.) He was required to allow a Church of England clergyman to establish a church in Pennsylvania if 20 or more colonists requested it, but this provision did not bother Penn, since he planned to offer complete religious freedom to all. In fact, he called

An engraving (c. 1752) of the gridlike street plan devised for the city of Philadelphia by William Penn and his surveyor general, Thomas Holme. Such advance planning was unique for its day; the pattern was copied by many towns and cities as America expanded westward.

the establishment of Pennsylvania a "Holy Experiment" in which he would attempt to embody God's will in an earthly place. Believing that God intended all men to live together in harmony and mutual toleration, Penn hoped to achieve these conditions in Pennsylvania. The colony was to be a sort of utopia, a Greek word meaning "no place" coined by Sir Thomas More in his 1516 book about an ideal and imaginary world. Penn intended—with God's help—to turn his version of utopia into reality.

One of Penn's first acts was to appoint his cousin William Markham as deputy governor. Markham sailed for Pennsylvania to begin building relationships with the Native American peoples who lived there and also with the thousand or so Europeans who had already settled in Pennsylvania. Most of these settlers were Dutch and Swedish, the remaining settlers from earlier colonizing ventures. Penn invited them to stay, and many of them did. These earlier settlers were the first of what would be the large and long-standing Dutch and Swedish communities of eastern Pennsylvania.

Penn also tried to attract settlers from Europe, chiefly from France, Germany, and the Netherlands. A number of Germans from a region called the Palatinate eventually did answer his call; most had met Penn or had heard him speak during his missionary tours. They formed the nucleus of a thriving German community in Pennsylvania. The community that is now called "Pennsylvania Dutch" was actually German in origin—the English colonists mistakenly called the Palatinate Germans "Dutch," and the name was handed down.

Penn was less successful in attracting colonists from France. He had hoped that French settlers would bring their silk-making and wine-making skills to Pennsylvania and establish industries there, but few French families came. He was pleased, nonetheless, that at least some colonists came from the European continent to join the Welsh, English, Scottish, and Irish settlers in the colony.

"THY GOD BRINGETH THEE INTO A GOOD LAND OF FOUNTAINS AND DEPTHS THAT SPRING OUT OF VALLEYS AND HILLS A LAND WHOSE STONES ARE IRON AND OUT OF WHOSE HILLS THOU MAYEST DIG BRASS"

He wanted people from different countries to live together amicably as part of his holy experiment. Settlement was slow at first, but the number of settlers soon increased, until by 1683 or 1684 at least one ship each week was bringing more members to the colony.

To Penn's delight, a great many of the colonists were craftspeople and congregated in villages and cities. He had been afraid that the colony would attract mostly farmers, who would settle on individual homesteads. While he realized that farming would necessarily be of great importance in Pennsylvania, he very much wanted to create a utopia that was partly urban rather than strictly rural. In fact,

An artist's view of Penn aboard the Welcome. *Penn and his companions did not leave England for America until September 1, 1682, more than a year after Penn was granted the land.*

PENNSYLVANIA: A PRIMER.

The FRAME of the
GOVERNMENT
OF THE
Province of Pennsilvania
IN
A M E R I C A :
Together with certain
L   A   W   S
Agreed upon in England
BY THE
GOVERNOUR
AND
Divers F R E E - M E N of the aforesaid
P R O V I N C E.

To be further Explained and Confirmed there by the first
Provincial Council and *General Assembly* that shall
be held, if they see meet.

Printed in the Year M DC LXXXII.
FAC-SIMILE OF TITLE PAGE OF PENN'S "FRAME OF GOVERNMENT, 1682.

Penn drew up The Frame of
the Government *for Pennsylvania to insure that he and
his successors would have
"no power of doing mischief,
so that the will of one man
may not hinder the good of
a whole country." A new
frame of government, the
Charter of Privileges, super-
seded it in 1701.*

Penn was a pioneering city planner who had spent a great deal of time visualizing his ideal city.

Painfully familiar with London and other European capitals where plague spread quickly through crowded slums and fires sometimes ravaged whole districts in a matter of hours, Penn wanted his capital to bring the healthfulness of country life into the city—an entirely new blend of both ways of life that he described as "a greene countrie towne, which will never be burned, and always be wholesome." Instead of narrow, twisting alleyways, he planned broad, tree-lined avenues running in a grid pattern along straight lines from north to south and from east to west. He included many parks, marketplaces, and squares, and each building would stand in the center of a lot containing a garden or orchard. Penn's capital, which he named Philadelphia (meaning "the city of brotherly love"), was the first American city to be laid out in advance, and its unique design was later emulated by many towns and cities as America's frontier moved westward.

In addition to city planning, Penn also engaged in social planning. He had many ideas that he wanted to put into practice in Pennsylvania. For one thing, he determined, all children from age 12 would be taught useful trades or skills. He also guaranteed the right of juries to return verdicts without fear of harassment—a lesson he had learned from his own trial with William Mead. Penn's own experiences also influenced his rules for imprisonment: all prisoners were to be treated well and provided with food and heat. And certain behaviors and activities, such as drunkenness, cursing, gambling, stage performances, lying, and gossiping were prohibited throughout the colony.

From these restrictions, we can see that Penn's idealistic belief in individual freedom sometimes came into conflict with his equally strong conviction that he knew the right way for others to live. He was so certain that his own ideas were best that he could not always resist the temptation to impose them upon others. This quality was evident

in the constitution, which outlined how the colony would
be governed. Three offical bodies were established in
Pennsylvania: the governor (Penn), the Council, and the
much larger General Assembly. Members of both the
Council and the General Assembly would be elected by
the vote of all adult male residents (women were not permitted to vote). Penn drew criticism from other liberal
thinkers, such as Algernon Sidney, who asserted that
Penn's arrangement, in which the Assembly could approve
or reject laws proposed by the Council but could neither
debate those proposals nor propose laws on its own, would
weaken the Assembly, the larger and therefore more representative house of the legislature. And some Quakers
pointed out that, as governor, Penn had reserved three
votes for himself, while everyone else was permitted only
one vote each; this scarcely meshed with the notion of uni-
versal equality. Others were disappointed that Penn had
not outlawed slavery or slave trading in Pennsylvania (a
1780 state law would provide for the gradual emancipation
of all slaves; slavery would not be legally abolished in
America until two centuries after Penn, in 1865).

Despite its flaws, however, Penn's system was extremely democratic by the standards of his time. It would be
unfair to judge Penn strictly by modern standards of
democracy, for although he was an enlightened and progressive thinker, he remained a man of his own era.

William Penn was, indeed, something of a paradox. He
devoted himself to the quest for religious liberation, yet
his idea of liberty could stretch only far enough to include
Christians; he would not allow atheists or Jews to vote or
hold office in Pennsylvania. And although he denounced
luxury and wrote earnest defenses of the simple, humble
life, he furnished his homes handsomely, dined well, and
never entirely abandoned a certain aristocratic gallantry
and flair in his dress and manners. To the end of his days,
he enjoyed associating with the learned and wellborn, and
he continued to feel that, as proprietor of Pennsylvania, he

Thomas Birch's rendering of William Penn's arrival in America, The Landing of William Penn *(c. 1850).*

had certain rights above those of ordinary colonists.

Penn's sense of overlordship was reflected in his treatment of rents and taxes in Pennsylvania. When Penn acquired the grant to Pennsylvania, he offered to sell parcels of land in two sizes: 5,000 acres and 750 acres. The buyers would also have to pay a tax called a quitrent, due each year beginning in 1684 on every 100 acres of land. In Penn's eyes, these taxes were no different from the rents paid by the tenants of his Shanagarry estate in

Ireland—as a symbol of his position as proprietor, they went into his personal income. But many of the settlers disagreed. They maintained that the purpose of the quitrents should be to pay for administrative costs, used for projects such as erecting public buildings, maintaining roads, and the like.

When it became clear that the colonial government would have to levy new taxes to pay these public expenses, the settlers demanded that Penn pay them out of the quitrents. Penn refused, and the question of whether or not the colony was obligated to provide Penn with an income vexed relations between the settlers and their governor for years. Ultimately, Penn was disappointed that the Pennsylvania colony did not enrich his personal fortune as he had hoped it would. This is another example of Penn's complex motives: to him, Pennsylvania was both a "holy experiment" and a money-making business venture.

Immediately after he was granted the Pennsylvania charter by King Charles, Penn published several pamphlets describing the many virtues of the new colony. He wrote at length about Pennsylvania's geography, climate, wildlife and vegetation, and native peoples. This wealth of information was so impressive that Penn was elected to the Royal Society, England's most prestigious association of learned men. Later travelers would find, however, that not all of the information Penn published was accurate. Having not yet visited his new landholding, he had in fact compiled it from a variety of sources. But in 1682, not long after the death of his mother, he sailed to America. Guli was in poor health, so she stayed in England with the children. Penn embarked in August on a small ship appropriately called the *Welcome*.

The dismal crossing lasted about two months. Smallpox broke out aboard ship. Having survived the disease as a child, Penn was immune to it, so he was able to help nurse the sick. But many of the passengers died. He was greatly relieved to step ashore in America, not far from the mouth of the Delaware River. Thomas Birch, an early 18th-century American painter, captured this historic moment in a painting called *The Landing of William Penn*, which portrays a neatly dressed and wigged Quaker extending the hand of friendship to a tomahawk-bearing Indian on a wooded, deserted shore. (Like other images of Penn in America, however, this painting owes more to imagination than to fact. Penn came ashore briefly at the small settlement of New Castle, where some of the European settlers lived; however, no records exist of Indians being present.) He then went back aboard the *Welcome* and sailed upriver to the site of Philadelphia. From there, he issued a summons to all colonists to meet in March 1683 in Philadelphia to agree on the constitution he had prepared.

Before the assembly, Penn toured the neighboring colonies of New York and New Jersey. He also chose a site for his personal estate: a wooded plot of 8,400 acres, situated on a bend in the Delaware River 26 miles north of Philadelphia, not far from the present-day city of Trenton, New Jersey. As part of his plan to establish fair and equal relationships with the Native Americans who lived in his colony, Penn purchased the property from the local Leni-Lenape Indians rather than simply seizing it, as most European settlers would. He began working on plans for an estate that he would call Pennsbury Manor.

The March 1683 meeting of the colonists did not go as smoothly as Penn had expected. The Assembly demanded the right to create and debate bills. The Council asked why Penn was allotted three votes when everyone else had only one. And Penn was disappointed to discover that only about half of the colonists were Quakers and that not all of them agreed with his plans and rules. The governor and the colonists agreed to draw up a new constitution giving the Assembly the power to write its own bills—but only with the Council's permission. The new document also stated that the colony's proprietor did not have to pay the costs of operating the government, a point that would continue to

A view of the herb garden at Pennsbury Manor, Penn's personal estate. The garden was recreated when the manor was rebuilt in the 1940s.

draw debate for many years. In the end, no one was completely satisfied with the second constitution. Nevertheless, it was adopted in April 1683.

Penn faced another problem, concerning Pennsylvania's border with Maryland. He and Lord Baltimore, the proprietor of Maryland, disagreed over the boundary lines between their two colonies. The charters granted to each of them were in great conflict: Lord Baltimore claimed that his charter included Delaware and a portion of southern Pennsylvania that encompassed the site chosen for Philadelphia. They agreed to let the king decide the matter, but the dispute turned into a frustrating and drawn-out affair that would not be fully settled during Penn's lifetime.

While awaiting the king's decision, Penn made an extensive circuit of his colony, visiting the Native Ameri-

Benjamin West's painting, William Penn's Treaty with the Indians, *1771–72, is believed to be a symbolic representation of the event.*

can peoples living in the area. He was more respectful of their cultures than most Europeans of his time, making a point of paying for land the settlers occupied. As a result of Penn's overtures, relations between whites and Native Americans were more amicable in Pennsylvania than in any other American colony.

Legend says that Penn signed a treaty of friendship with the Delaware Indians at a place called Shackamaxon, just north of Philadelphia. This event is depicted in *William Penn's Treaty with the Indians*, a well-known painting by

Benjamin West, an 18th-century American painter who became popular in England. Although the painting includes probably the most familiar image of Penn, it cannot be regarded as a true portrait because it was painted in 1773, many years after Penn's death. The work also contains anachronisms, such as the inclusion of people who could not have been present in Shackamaxon in the 1680s wearing a style of clothing that had not yet been designed. Finally, the incident itself probably did not occur at the time and place suggested in the painting. Penn and the Delaware Indians did have a treaty, but the time and place of its signing are unknown. Nevertheless, West's painting exemplifies the reverence with which Americans still viewed William Penn nearly a century after he founded Pennsylvania.

Penn had hoped to make a long stay in his colony and to send for his family to join him. But in the summer of 1684 he was forced to return to London on urgent business. He not only wanted to press the king to settle the boundary dispute with Lord Baltimore, he was also worried about the very survival of his charter. Royal officials had caught several French ships trading with the American colonists. This was in violation of the colonial charters, which forbade the colonists to deal with any but British traders. A growing faction of the royal court insisted that the individual proprietors could not maintain sufficient control over their colonies and that all the charters should be withdrawn, placing British America fully under the control of the Crown. Penn hastened back to England to try to stop this threatening idea from gaining force. When he stepped aboard the vessel *Endeavour* for the homeward voyage, he did not suspect that it would be 15 years before he would see his colony again.

This engraving of William Penn holding the deed to his American land is typical of the way in which artists have portrayed the proprietor of Pennsylvania.

7

THE PROPRIETOR
OF PENN'S WOODS

THE YEARS FOLLOWING Penn's return to England were frequently sad and difficult. He encountered trouble and disappointment on four fronts: political events in England, differences of opinion with the Pennsylvania colonists, worsening financial troubles, and family problems.

To Penn's dismay, he learned that Quakers were being vigorously persecuted in England. He was himself fined or arrested several times for speaking at Quaker meetings. But although he protested to the king, Charles II was dying and had little time to worry about the treatment of the Nonconformists. When James, the duke of York, succeeded to the throne, he promised his old friend Penn that he would free the Quakers from jail and make life easier for all Nonconformists.

The duke was crowned King James II in February 1685, but he was unable to do as much for the Nonconformists as Penn had hoped. James was a Catholic ruler in a strongly anti-Catholic nation. Many of the king's subjects suspected that he was plotting to restore Catholic supremacy in England, and any toleration he showed for the Noncon-

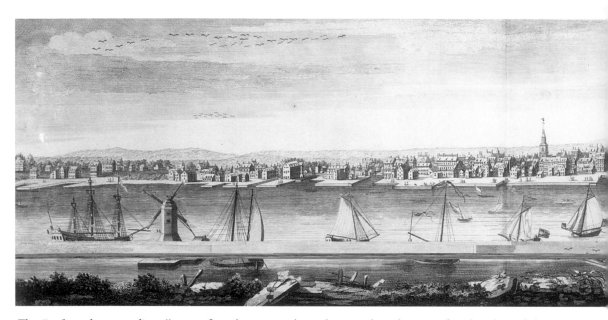

The "safe and commodious" harbor of Philadelphia, viewed from New Jersey across the Delaware River. By 1753, the date of this engraving, Philadelphia had grown into a thriving trade town of "near two thousand three hundred" residents, and was hailed for its spacious streets and protected location.

formists was viewed as paving the way for the rise of the Catholics. People reasoned that if the king allowed the Quakers and other Protestant Nonconformists to have rights, the Catholics might take advantage of them as well. And because William Penn worked tirelessly for religious freedom, old accusations that he was a secret Catholic were revived. Even some his of fellow Quakers in England and Pennsylvania began to believe these rumors, and they wished that Penn would distance himself from King James, for they, too, feared a Catholic return to power.

James remained on the throne for less than four years. In 1688, driven largely by the fear of Catholicism, the people and parliament of England demanded that he step down. Unlike the Civil War that had wracked the country a generation earlier, James's fall from power was bloodless. He quietly went into exile, and the throne of England was turned over to a Protestant European prince, William of Orange, and his wife, Mary, who was next in line to ascend the English throne.

William and Mary ushered in a new era of religious liberty with the Act of Toleration, which was passed in 1689.

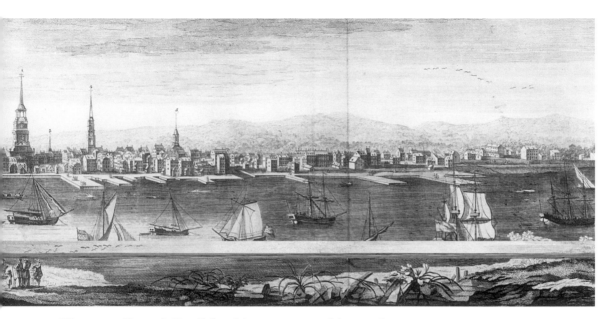

The act allowed English citizens to worship as they pleased without fear of punishment. Although some restrictions on holding public office still remained in force, the Act of Toleration was a milestone in the development of human rights and a model for similar laws in other countries. Much of the credit for its passing goes to William Penn, who had argued for more than 20 years that people whose beliefs placed them outside the state's established church did not automatically pose a threat to order and security and that these people deserved the same rights as everyone else. Penn himself was not well liked by King William and Queen Mary, however, mostly because he stubbornly refused to renounce his friendship with the exiled James, with whom he still corresponded. Indeed, Penn was kept under surveillance by royal agents until William and Mary decided that he was not a spy for James.

At the same time, Penn was struggling to maintain control of Pennsylvania. He had sent a succession of deputy governors to the colony, but none was effective and most were resented and mistrusted by the colonists. Even Penn's one success was not an easy victory: the royal court had upheld his claim against Lord Baltimore and had assigned the three counties on the border between the two colonies to Pennsylvania. However, disputes over the land continued. These counties remained rebellious for some time, and they occasionally threatened to withdraw from the colony.

Penn faced more serious problems with Pennsylvania as well. The Board of Trade and Plantations, a council that managed the affairs of the colonies under the control of the Crown, claimed that privately owned colonies such as Penn's were inefficient. The lords commissioners of the Board wanted to revoke, or cancel, the various charters and bring all colonies under their unified administration. In an attempt to avert this crisis, Penn proposed to the people of all the American colonies that they voluntarily form a union to cooperate in certain matters: to agree on a common currency, to control smuggling and other crimes, and if necessary, to prepare for their common defense against an attack by France or another hostile foreign power. In short, Penn's 1697 proposal, called *A Brief and Plain Scheme for Union*, was one of the earliest suggestions that the colonies unite and take on the responsibilities of self-government. And although he did not go so far as to suggest independence from England, Penn's notion of unity did foreshadow the concept of an American nation. But his call went unheard. Most colonists did not trust those in other colonies, and the idea of mutual cooperation was ignored.

The lords commissioners of trade and plantations were particularly angry about the amount of smuggling and illegal foreign trade that was going on in Pennsylvania (and in other colonies as well). In letter after letter, Penn urged the Council and the Assembly to enforce the trade laws, but the colonists did not take the matter seriously and nothing happened. Penn grew so frustrated that he threatened to revoke the constitution and rule the colony personally— another instance in which his belief in the ability of the

ordinary man to govern himself wisely collided with the unpalatable fact that people did not always do what he expected them to do.

Relations between Penn and the colony's other officials grew worse when war loomed between England and France. The French, who owned a large colony in Canada, had made allies among some Native American tribes, and England feared that a combined French and Indian force would attack the English colonies. (This did happen, but not until the middle of the 18th century.) Nearly every year, the Board of Trade and Plantations asked the colonies to contribute volunteers and funds for a militia, or armed force, to defend against possible attacks by the French or the Indians. Since the threat usually lay near the northern border of New York, far from Pennsylvania, the

William Penn and Hannah Callowhill are married in a Friends ceremony two years after the death of Penn's first wife, Guli. Penn and Hannah were survived by three sons, John, Thomas, and Richard.

The "Letitia House" in Philadelphia was the first brick building erected in the city. Penn gave the home to his daughter, Letitia.

Pennsylvanians felt little pressure to contribute. Further-more, the Quaker population of the colony maintained that supporting a militia clashed with their principles of nonviolence, and they refused to contribute. But Penn's charter, like all of the colonial charters, required the colonists upon request of the Crown to contribute toward their own defense. The Board of Trade and Plantations seized upon Pennsylvania's refusal as evidence that the colony was badly managed.

The issue of defense greatly troubled the colony's proprietor. Penn was still a passionate believer in nonviolence. In 1693 he published an important book called *An Essay Toward the Present and Future Peace of Europe* that anticipated the establishment of the United Nations by two and one-half centuries. Penn called for an international parliament, where nations could settle their disputes without going to war. In this, as in so many other ideas, Penn was ahead of his time. But his proposal was disregarded. The problem of colonial defense did not go away, however, and Penn was forced to admit that under the charter he was responsible for enforcing the law. He was sometimes able to browbeat the reluctant colonists into paying the militia tax, but the amount fell short every year. To save his charter, Penn had to make up the difference out of his own pocket.

That pocket was no longer as deep as it had been. For Penn, Pennsylvania was a constant expense that brought no income; sales of land in Pennsylvania had tapered off, and the colonists balked at paying their quitrents. Furthermore, Ireland was once again wracked by uprisings and rebellions, which kept Penn from collecting his rents from Shanagarry.

Penn, who had grown up in a wealthy family and had never known poverty, sometimes displayed a casual attitude toward his own debts. He would acknowledge that he owed money to others, but he hated being asked to pay off his debts before he was ready. In the late 1680s, however, his creditors grew insistent. Among them was Philip Ford, Penn's former steward at Shanagarry who also had been his business manager for many years. Not only did Penn owe Ford an amount equal to several years' worth of his own salary, but he had also borrowed money from Ford. Now Ford pressed Penn for payment on these debts—with interest due. The amount came to nearly 4,300 pounds, a huge sum (by comparison, Penn sold 5,000-acre tracts in Pennsylvania for 100 pounds each).

Penn was gravely disappointed by Ford's lack of trust; he seemed unable to understand that Ford genuinely expected to receive the money. Finally, the two men agreed on a complicated system of mortgages that gave Penn an extended time to pay his debts and granted Ford a

A contemporary view of Pennsbury Manor. After Penn's death, the estate's main buildings fell into disrepair and by 1929 all of the original structures were gone. The manor house, outbuildings, and landscape were restored between 1933 and 1942, according to Penn's original instructions.

claim on the charter of Pennsylvania as security. Ford drew up the agreement, and Penn, never a prudent businessman, signed it without reading it—a rash act that caused serious problems a few years later.

The defense crisis came to a head in 1693. Penn's enemies on the Board of Trade and Plantations convinced King William that Pennsylvania's lack of a militia was a military danger. William suspended Penn's right to govern the colony and placed Pennsylvania under the command of New York. Penn's charter was restored in 1694, but only after the Pennsylvania Assembly passed a law that levied a militia tax.

Penn's personal life was filled with grief during these years. His dearly beloved wife, Gulielma Penn, died in

1694 at age 50, and after her death Penn himself was seriously ill for several months. His life took a positive turn two years later, when he married Hannah Callowhill, the daughter of a pious Quaker acquaintance. Although Hannah was 24 years younger than Penn, their marriage was happy. A shrewd and practical businesswoman, Hannah Penn helped her husband manage his increasingly tangled financial affairs. But Penn's joy in his new marriage was marred by the death of his elder son, Springett, just five weeks after the wedding.

Springett Penn, following in his father's footsteps, had been a devout Quaker. The same could not be said of Penn's surviving son, William Jr., who was called Billy. Impatient with Quaker plainness, Billy Penn ran up debts and made friends among a wild, loose-living set of young men. He married at age 17, and although Penn wanted him to take a hand in managing Pennsylvania, Billy refused to settle in what he thought was a wilderness. A few years later, in a curious echo of Penn's struggles with his own father, Billy was offered the captaincy of an Irish regiment. Penn proudly ordered him to turn it down; it was not good enough for a Penn, he declared.

Through all these years of trouble and turmoil, Penn yearned to return to Pennsylvania. At last, with his business affairs somewhat stable and his charter as secure as he could make it, he sailed for America in September 1699 with his new wife. In January 1700, two months after arriving in Pennsylvania, Hannah gave birth to a boy they named John—the first Penn born in Pennsylvania.

Penn was most eager to settle into Pennsbury Manor. The home had been built while he was in England, according to his detailed instructions—which called for large and beautiful gardens. But there was much work for him in the capital of Pennsylvania, whose population had grown to more than 5,000, second in size among American cities only to Boston, Massachusetts. Penn was saddened to see that Philadelphia's rapid growth had caused some of his precious schemes for parks and yards to be abandoned. Although broad boulevards and green areas remained, some districts of the city had become crowded and almost slumlike. His first priority, however, was strengthening the enforcement of the trade laws.

As he set about tidying up the disorder in Pennsylvania's administration, Penn learned that the colonists were as unhappy with his governorship as he was with them, and that the Council and the Assembly were divided into quarrelsome factions. This is common with governmental bodies, but the situation depressed Penn, who was growing weary of the constant struggle to impose his ideas. Together, he and the colonists developed a third constitution, which they called the Charter of Privileges. It eliminated the Council and created a larger Assembly, which became the sole lawmaking body of the colony. The new charter also granted the governor the power to veto acts passed by the Assembly. The only laws that were not changed were those that guaranteed religious liberty.

The Charter of Privileges created a balance of power in which the governor and the Assembly could act independently, but neither could compel the other to act against its will. The charter took effect in 1701 and continued in force until the American Revolution of the 1770s. It is thought to have contributed to the checks-and-balances system of the United States Constitution.

After April 1701, Penn and his family lived at Pennsbury. The mansion was furnished with elegant imported goods and staffed by numerous slaves and servants, leading many in the colony to remark that Penn lived richly for a simple Quaker. But Penn saw no contradiction between comfort and piety. As proprietor of the colony and a wellborn individual, he felt entitled to a certain standard of living—and he was paying for it himself, after all. He hosted many splendid dinner parties in the paneled dining room at Pennsbury; among his guests were local Indian chiefs. Some of Penn's surviving letters show that he and Hannah sent to town for supplies such as bricks, lime, locks, and nails, and for provisions such as chocolate, flour, bacon, coffee, and corn meal. But like the Wanstead estate where Penn had grown up, Pennsbury was practically self-sufficient, with its own vineyard, orchard, farm, beehives, cemetery, bakery, brewery, and smokehouse for preserving meat. Located in a wild area far from other habitations and easily accessible only by water, the manor had to produce most of its own provisions. But Penn loved the solitude and natural beauty there. One of his favorite pastimes was walking in the garden, where he had cultivated rare plants imported from Europe and the West Indies. He also loved traveling to Philadelphia and back on the Delaware River in a large boat that he called his barge.

By the time the Charter of Privileges had been written, the Board of Trade and Plantations was threatening to revoke Penn's own charter to the Pennsylvania colony, so once more he went to London to do battle with the lords commissioners. He departed from Philadelphia in November 1701, intending to be away only a short time before settling for good in Pennsylvania. But he would never return. In two visits, Penn had spent a total of about four years in the colony he had created.

Penn's "greene countrie towne" of Philadelphia retains some of the broad, tree-lined avenues planned by its founder. The Benjamin Franklin Parkway, shown here, runs through Logan Circle, one of Penn's original five parks, and connects City Hall to the Philadelphia Museum of Art (upper left).

8

PENN'S LEGACY

AS WITH HIS earlier trip to London, Penn arrived to face a sea of troubles. One of the biggest issues concerned freedom of religion. There was a very real danger that the Act of Toleration would be revoked and that Nonconformists and Dissenters would again suffer fierce persecution. Some Friends even feared that Quakerism would be extinguished. Penn's life work, it seemed, might have been in vain.

The cause of all this worry was a princess named Anne, the younger sister of Queen Mary. Anne was a strict Anglican and strongly disapproved of Nonconformism. After she assumed the throne in March 1702, Penn wrote a letter telling the queen about the loyalty of "the people commonly called Quakers" and urging her to support the Act of Toleration. Whether she was moved by Penn's appeal or by more general considerations of policy, Anne responded graciously. "[Y]ou and your friends may be assured of my protection," she wrote to Penn, and she promised that the Act of Toleration would never be repealed.

Penn had less success in other areas. His son Billy had finally agreed to go to Pennsylvania and take up some administrative duties, but Billy proved careless and ineffective. Moreover, he made himself unpopular with the colonists by brawling in taverns, and he offended the pacifist Quakers by forming his own militia. Penn ordered him back to England in 1705, and Billy gave formal notice that he no longer considered himself a Quaker. Penn, who had spent a lifetime preaching the right of each individual to make his own religious decisions, had great difficulty accepting Billy's decision. His disappointment was reflected in his will, which left Billy the Irish estate but divided Pennsylvania among John, Thomas, and Richard, his three sons by Hannah.

Another problem for Penn was the matter of the money he owed to Philip Ford. When Ford died, his widow sued Penn for more than 11,000 pounds and threatened to claim ownership of Pennsylvania if he did not pay. The badly worded agreement Penn had signed with Ford a few years earlier gave his widow a disputable claim to the colony. Penn was forced to spend nine months in debtors' prison in 1707–08 for failing to pay the Ford family. He hired lawyers to sort out the mess, and finally the Fords agreed to accept 7,600 pounds as full payment. Penn raised the sum by borrowing from friends and by mortgaging lots in Pennsylvania.

Meanwhile, the Pennsylvania Assembly had grown lazy about collecting taxes and quitrents. The issue of defense money and militias also continued to cause trouble with the Board of Trade and Plantations. It seemed to Penn that the colonists argued with everything he tried to do. Profoundly frustrated, in 1703 he decided to wash his hands of the whole colony. He offered to sell back his charter to the lords commissioners for 40,000 pounds. However, the Board found the price—and the long list of privileges that Penn insisted on retaining—unacceptable, and the proposal went no further.

After the Ford claim was settled, Penn returned briefly to a life he loved. He spent part of 1709 and 1710 traveling through England, speaking at Quaker meetings, mak-

ing converts, and holding theological debates. In such activities, he found a calmness and certainty that he had never enjoyed as a colonial proprietor. Whatever his problems might be, as a missionary Penn was sure that he was doing God's will.

By now, however, the energy that had powered his life of service began to wane. Like his father, Penn suffered from gout, which often kept him bedridden for weeks at a time. He also endured several sharp attacks of something referred to as "fever," which may in fact have been minor strokes. In early 1710 he went home and gathered his family around him. He did little traveling thereafter.

Once again he tried to sell his charter back to Great Britain. Pennsylvania had become for Penn nothing more than a financial drain and a constant source of worry. The

William Penn and many of his family members, including his wives, are buried in the grave-yard of Jordans Meeting House in Buckinghamshire, England.

"holy experiment" had not turned out quite as he had planned, and he was willing to separate himself from it and leave the colonists to work out their own destiny. After renewing negotiations with the queen's representatives, he agreed in 1712 to accept 12,000 pounds for Pennsylvania. But before the contract could be completed, Penn suffered a severe stroke that left him confused and partially paralyzed. Because he was unable to conduct business, the sale was postponed.

Penn never regained enough strength or mental powers to complete the agreement. He remained the proprietor of Pennsylvania in name, and Hannah Penn took over the correspondence and other duties involved in long-distance administration. Although she proved a capable manager, the Pennsylvania Assembly had achieved a fairly high degree of independence, and most of the time it simply made its own decisions. The Penn family's ownership of the colony was increasingly regarded as a courtesy rather than a controlling factor in Pennsylvania's government.

Penn grew weaker and more confused as the years passed. Hannah tended to him affectionately, but he had entered a long, gentle decline. For some time, he was unable to recognize old friends, to attend Quaker meetings, or to debate any of the philosophical issues to which he had devoted so many years of his life. He died on July 30, 1718, and was buried in the Quaker cemetery in Jordans, Buckinghamshire, in England.

Penn's son Billy died two years after his father; Hannah Penn died in 1726. Penn's descendants retained the official proprietorship of Pennsylvania until the American Revolution nullified all colonial charters with Great Britain.

Penn's legacy lives on in Pennsylvania, which is still called the Quaker State. The Quaker heritage is felt especially in the Philadelphia area, where many Friends have become prominent in business and politics and where Friends schools are among the city's finest. Pennsbury Manor, which fell into ruin after the Penns died, has been

A watercolor by American artist N. C. Wyeth depicts the dreams and accomplishments of Pennsylvania's founder.

restored to its original state and now serves as a Penn museum. Vestiges of the "greene countrie towne" that Penn planned are still evident in Philadelphia, which has one of the country's largest urban park systems. Atop Philadelphia's city hall stands a 37-foot-tall bronze statue of the state's founder, cast in 1893 by the sculptor Alexander Milne Calder. The figure, holding a charter in one hand, gazes broodingly down on the City of Brotherly Love, whose residents treat "Billy Penn" with familiar affection. (While the building underwent extensive renovations in the 1980s, citizens passed out "Free Billy Penn" buttons to alert others that the statue had been imprisoned for too long by scaffolding; and Penn's likeness is often dressed in jerseys or hats featuring the logos of local professional sports teams that are bound for playoff games.)

Penn also exerted a powerful influence on the formation of the United States. At a time when few thinkers ventured to discuss religious liberty, government by representation, and respect for individual freedom, Penn gave voice to these and other liberal concepts that came to be seen as distinctively American values. Thomas Jefferson, one of America's founding fathers, called Penn "the greatest lawgiver the world has produced."

Penn's decent treatment of Native Americans also set an example—one that was not, unfortunately, followed in many other areas of the country. And Penn encouraged a greater degree of ethnic and cultural diversity than any other colony in America could claim.

But Penn's most important legacy reaches far beyond the founding of Pennsylvania: his commitment to the rights of conscience—the right of the individual to choose his own faith, to refrain from making war, and to preach and write freely. Penn was not completely free of prejudices, nor did he always manage to follow his own principles without compromise. But he made a conscious, daily effort to live the best life he could, hoping to inspire others to do likewise.

Penn was a singularly enlightened and compassionate man, not only for his own time, but for all times. In 1693 he summed up his beliefs in this way: "Love is above all; and when it prevails in us all, we shall all be Lovely and in Love with God and with one another."

The 37-foot-tall bronze sculpture of William Penn, created by the sculptor Alexander Milne Calder, stands outside City Hall before being raised atop its tower. The building was completed in 1901.

APPENDIX

PENN'S LEGACY OF RELIGIOUS FREEDOM: PHILADELPHIA HISTORIC SITES

Arch Street Friends Meeting House, the oldest meeting house in Philadelphia and the largest in the world. 320 Arch Street, Philadelphia PA. 215-627-2667.

Christ Church, built 1727–1754 and containing the "600-year-old font" from England in which Penn was baptized. Second and Market Streets, Philadelphia PA. 215-922-1695.

City Hall, topped by Alexander Milne Calder's bronze sculpture of William Penn; the statue faces northeast toward Penn Treaty Park, the site where Penn is said to have negotiated his final agreement with the local Native Americans. Penn Square, at intersection of Broad and Market Streets, Philadelphia PA.

Congregation Mikveh Israel, one of the oldest Jewish congregations in the United States. 44 North 4th Street, Philadelphia PA. 215-922-5446. http://www.libertynet.org/~kkmi

Free Quaker Meeting House, founded in 1783 by Quakers who were "read out of meeting" for assisting in the American Revolution. Arch Street between 5th and 6th Streets, Philadelphia PA.

Historic St. George's United Methodist Church, called the "cradle of American Methodism," the world's oldest Methodist church in continuous service. 235 North 4th Street, Philadelphia PA. 215-925-7788.

Mother Bethel African Methodist Episcopal Church, founded by Richard Allen, the second oldest black congregation in the country, situated on the oldest parcel of real estate continuously owned by African Americans. 419 Richard Allen Avenue (Lombard Street between 5th and 6th Streets), Philadelphia PA. 215-925-0616.

Old First Reformed Church, one of the earliest German Reformed Churches in America. The charter under which the church operates was granted by William Penn's sons Thomas and Richard. 4th and Race Streets, Philadelphia PA. 215-922-4566.

Old Pine Street Presbyterian Church, called the "Church of the Patriots." The land on which it stands was purchased from William Penn's sons Thomas and Richard. 412 Pine Street, Philadelphia PA. 215-925-8051. http://www.libertynet.org/~oldpine/

Old St. Augustine's Church, once home to the "sister" of the Liberty Bell (a replacement bell ordered when the original cracked), which was destroyed by fire during the 1840s. 4th and New Streets, Philadelphia PA. 215-627-3911.

Old St. Joseph's Church, founded in 1733; the oldest Roman Catholic Church in Philadelphia. 321 Willings Alley, Philadelphia, PA. 215-923-1733. http://www.sju.edu/~osj/

Old St. Mary's Church, Philadelphia's first Roman Catholic cathedral, site of the first public religious commemoration of the Declaration of Independence. 252 South 4th Street, Philadelphia PA. 215-923-7930.

Pennsbury Manor, the Pennsylvania home of William Penn. 400 Pennsbury Memorial Road, Morrisville, PA. 215-946-0400. http://www.libertynet.org/~pensbury

Penn's Landing, encompassing the spot where William Penn first touched ground; today a riverside park and summer concert venue. Columbus Avenue (formerly Delaware

Avenue) between South and Vine Streets, Philadelphia, PA.

St. Peter's Church, built by the Church of England, completed in 1761. 313 Pine Street, Philadelphia, PA. 215-925-5968.

Society Hill, named for the Free Society of Traders, a stock company to whom William Penn granted land and privileges. Extending from 2nd to 5th Street and from Walnut to Lombard Streets, Philadelphia, PA.

Washington Square, one of the five original squares laid out in William Penn's plan for the "green country towne"; originally called Southeast Square (Quakers did not believe in naming places after people); on its edge was the site of the Orange Street Friends' Meeting House. Bounded by 6th and 7th Streets and by Walnut and South Seventh Street, Philadelphia, PA.

Welcome Park, the only site in historic Philadelphia dedicated to the life and contributions of William Penn; contains a marble replica of Penn's original city plan and a small copy of the William Penn sculpture atop City Hall. William Penn's son, John, was born on this site. Second Street and Sansom Street Alley, Philadelphia, PA.

Wyck House, one of the oldest surviving buildings in the Philadelphia area, owned and lived in by nine generations of one Quaker family. 6026 Germantown Avenue, Philadelphia, PA. 215-848-1690. http://pobox.upenn.edu/~converse/

OTHER LINKS:

History of Manayunk, PA (land granted by Penn):
http://www.gim.net/gic/north_america/usa/pennsylvania/philadelphia/manayunk/history/

Pennsylvania Dutch Country Welcome Center (Lancaster County, PA):
http://www.800padutch.com/

Quaker Resources: http://www.quaker.org/

Religious Tolerance: http://www.religioustolerance.org/

FURTHER READING

Bronner, Edwin B. *William Penn's Holy Experiment: The Founding of Philadelphia, 1681–1701*. Philadelphia: Temple University Press, 1962.

———. *William Penn, 17th Century Founding Father: Selections from His Political Writings*. Wallingford, Pa.: Pendle Hill, 1975.

Buranelli, Vincent. *The King and the Quaker: A Study of William Penn and James II*. Philadelphia: University of Pennsylvania Press, 1962.

Burt, Struthers. *Philadelphia: Holy Experiment*. Garden City, N.Y.: Doubleday, 1945.

Dunn, Mary Maples. *William Penn: Politics and Conscience*. Princeton, N.J.: Princeton University Press, 1967.

Fantel, Hans. *William Penn: Apostle of Dissent*. New York: Morrow, 1974.

Foster, Genevieve. *The World of William Penn*. New York: Scribners, 1973.

Fradin, Dennis B. *The Pennsylvania Colony*. Chicago: Children's Press, 1988.

Gray, Elizabeth J. *Penn*. New York: Viking, 1938.

Illick, Joseph. *William Penn the Politician: His Relations with the English Government*. Ithaca, N.Y.: Cornell University Press, 1967.

Soderland, Jean, ed. *William Penn and the Founding of Pennsylvania: A Documentary History*. Philadelphia: University of Pennsylvania Press and Historical Society of Pennsylvania, 1983.

Stevens, S. K. *The Pennsylvania Colony*. London: Collier-Macmillan, 1970.

Tolles, Frederick, and Gordon Alderfer, eds. *The Witness of William Penn*. New York: Macmillan, 1957.

Trussell, John B., Jr. *William Penn: Architect of a Nation*. Harrisburg, Pa.: Pennsylvania Historical and Museum Commission, 1980.

Wildes, Harry Emerson. *William Penn*. New York: Macmillan, 1974.

CHRONOLOGY

1642–51	English Civil War pits Royalists against Parliamentarians
1644	William Penn born on October 14 in London, England
1649	King Charles I executed by Parliamentarians; England declared a commonwealth
1653	Oliver Cromwell named Lord Protector of the Commonwealth
1658	Cromwell dies; his son, Richard, succeeds him
1660	English monarchy restored when Charles II assumes British throne William Penn attends college in Oxford but leaves during his second year
1662–64	Penn travels and studies in France and travels to Italy with Robert Spencer
1665	Penn serves briefly in the Royal Navy London is ravaged by an outbreak of bubonic plague
1666	The Great Fire sweeps through London, destroying 80 percent of the city Penn goes to Ireland to manage family property
1667	Penn joins the Friends of Truth (Quakers) and is jailed for attending a Quaker meeting in Cork
1668	Penn is imprisoned in the Tower of London for treason following the publication of his religious pamphlet *Sandy Foundations Shaken*
1669	Penn writes *No Cross, No Crown* about Quaker and Puritan beliefs
1670	Penn is arrested for preaching in the street and acquitted after a landmark controversial trial
1671	While in jail again for refusing to swear an oath, Penn writes *The Great Case of Liberty of Conscience* about religious toleration; after his release from prison, Penn travels through the Netherlands and Germany seeking converts to Quakerism
1672	Penn marries Gulielma Springett
1674	Penn becomes involved with a Quaker colony in New Jersey
1677	Penn and other Quakers travel to the Netherlands, Belgium, and Germany on a missionary tour

1681	Charles II grants the large American colony of Pennsylvania to Penn
1682	Penn travels to Pennsylvania to preside over first assembly of the "holy experiment"
1684	Penn returns to England to negotiate the Maryland-Pennsylvania boundary with the king
1685	James II, brother of Charles II, becomes king
1688	James II is deposed; William of Orange and his wife, Mary, become joint sovereigns
1689	The Act of Toleration is passed in England, broadening religious liberty
1693	Penn writes *An Essay Toward the Present and Future Peace of Europe*, calling for an international parliament
1693–94	Penn falls out of favor with the court and temporarily loses title to the Pennsylvania colony
1694	Penn's wife, Gulielma, dies
1696	Penn marries Hannah Callowhill
1699	Penn returns to America to head the Pennsylvania colony
1700	Penn and his family move to Pennsbury Manor, outside of Philadelphia
1701	A constitution called the *Charter of Privileges* becomes law in Pennsylvania; Penn leaves the colony for England
1702	Anne, daughter of James II, assumes the British throne
1703	Penn attempts to sell the Pennsylvania colony to the British government
1712	Penn makes a deal with the British government and begins preparations to sell Pennsylvania, but he suffers a stroke and the sale is postponed, never to be completed
1718	After several years as an invalid, Penn dies on July 30 and is buried in Buckinghamshire, England

INDEX

Act of Toleration, 86–87, 97

Amyraut, Moïse, 43, 55, 61

Anne (queen of England), 97

Anglican Church. *See* Church of England

Anglo-Dutch Wars, 44, 45, 47–48

Billinge, Edward, 68, 69

Birch, Thomas, 80

Board of Trade and Plantations, 88, 90, 92, 95, 98

Brief and Plain Scheme for Union, A, 88

Bushell, Edward, 64–66

Calder, Alexander Milne, 102

Charles I (king of England), 20, 22, 25, 37

Charles II (king of England), 12, 25, 31, 32, 33, 35, 37, 38–39, 44, 47–48, 62, 72, 73, 79, 85

Chigwell Free Grammar School, 28–29

Christ Church College, 36, 41

Church of England, 21, 22, 28, 29, 38, 43, 53, 55, 61, 62, 73

Civil War, English, 20–26, 86

Coale, Josiah, 56, 59, 72

Congreve, William, 37

Cooke, Francis, 61

Cromwell, Oliver, 22, 25–26, 30–31, 32, 35

Dissenters, 21, 52, 62, 97

England, 11, 19, 21, 25, 26, 37, 44, 52, 63, 64, 65, 67, 68, 71, 72, 79, 85, 88, 98

Essay Toward the Present and Future Peace of Europe, An, 90–91

Fenwick, John, 68

Fifth Monarchists, the, 16, 52

Ford, Philip, 63, 91–92, 98

Foundation of God Standeth, The (Vincent), 61

Fox, George, 52, 53, 57, 59, 66, 67–68, 72

Great Case of Liberty of Conscience, The, 66

"Hat honor," 42–43, 52

Inner Light doctrine, 32, 52

Innocency with Its Open Face, 62

Inns of Court, 45

Ireland, 11, 12, 14, 16, 17, 21, 22, 23, 24, 25, 26, 31, 35, 49, 50, 51, 55, 63, 79, 91

James II (king of England), 39, 47, 49, 63, 72, 85, 87

Jefferson, Thomas, 102

Jenkins, Leoline, 72, 73

Lincoln's Inn, 45, 48

Loe, Thomas, 32, 51, 57, 59, 66

London, England, 22, 23, 26, 27, 31, 32, 35, 38, 40, 41, 44, 45, 47, 56, 57, 61, 63, 64, 95, 97

Great Fire of, 48–49

Great Plague of, 48, 49, 76

Louis XIV (king of France), 42, 44

Markham, William, 74

Mead, William, 63–66, 76

More, Thomas, 74

Native Americans, 73, 74, 80, 81–83, 89, 94, 102

Naylor, James, 55

No Cross, No Crown, 62

Nonconformists, 21, 32, 28, 49, 52, 55, 85, 86, 97

Oxford University, 36–41, 42, 44, 45

Owen, John, 38, 39–40, 41, 43, 55, 61

Penn, Gulielma Springett "Guli" (first wife), 28, 59–60, 62, 63, 67, 68, 79, 92–93

Penn, Hannah Callowhill (second wife), 93, 94, 100

Penn, John (son), 93, 98
Penn, Letitia (daughter), 68
Penn, Margaret Jasper
    Vanderschuren (moth-
    er), 23–24, 26, 28, 36,
    44, 79
Penn, Margaret "Pegg"
    (sister), 28
Penn, Richard (brother),
    28, 68
Penn, Richard (son), 98
Penn, Thomas (son), 98
Penn, William
    in America, 16, 79–83,
        93
    arrests and imprison-
        ments, 11–17, 31, 55,
        57, 60–62, 63–66, 76,
        98
    birth, 24
    childhood, 25, 26–31, 59
    death, 100
    in duel, 42–43, 52
    education, 28–30, 31,
        36–41, 45, 48
    European travels, 42–44,
        66, 72
    disagreements with
        father, 36–37, 40–42,
        48, 50, 55–57, 66, 93
    and individual rights, 16,
        17, 66, 69, 76, 87, 102
    legacy, 16, 97–103
    marriages, 63, 68, 93
    and Pennsylvania, 17,
        19, 41, 68–83, 86,
        87–91, 92, 93–95, 97,

98, 99, 100
    and Quakerism, 11–17,
        28, 31–32, 38, 43, 49,
        50, 51–55, 56–69, 80,
        85, 90, 93, 97, 98–99,
        100
    and religious freedom,
        16, 17, 21, 29, 41, 55,
        66, 69, 73, 77, 86, 102
    as soldier, 45, 47–48, 50
    writings, 16, 27, 38, 41,
        49, 57, 61, 62, 66, 79,
        88, 90–91
Penn, William (father), 12,
    14, 16, 17, 20–25, 26,
    30–36, 37, 38–39,
    40–42, 44, 45, 48, 49,
    50, 55–57, 62, 63, 64,
    65, 66, 93, 99
Penn, William, Jr. (son),
    68, 93, 97–98, 100
Pennington, Isaac, 28, 60
Pennsbury Manor, 80, 93,
    94, 95, 100–102
Pennsylvania, 17, 19, 41,
    68–83, 86, 87, 88, 89,
    90, 91, 92, 93–95, 97,
    98, 99, 100
Pepys, Samuel, 35–36, 42,
    44
Philadelphia, Pennsylva-
    nia, 76, 80, 81, 82, 95
Puritans, 13, 21, 22, 25, 26,
    28, 32, 37, 38, 52, 55

Quakerism, 11–17, 28,
    31–32, 38, 43, 49, 50,

51–55, 56–69, 80, 85,
    90, 97, 98–99, 100

Religious freedom, 16, 17,
    21, 29, 41, 55, 66, 69,
    73, 77, 86, 102
Roman Catholics, 13, 21,
    22, 24, 62, 63, 85, 86

Saltmarsh, John, 29
*Sandy Foundations
    Shaken*, 61, 62
Saumur, 43
Shanagarry, 35, 49, 56, 63,
    78, 91–92
Sidney, Algernon, 44, 71,
    77
Society of Friends. *See*
    Quakerism
Spencer, Robert, 44, 72
Starling, Samuel, 64–66
Stillingfleet, Edward,
    61–62

Test Act, the, 67
*Truth Rescued from Impos-
    tors*, 66

Vincent, Thomas, 60–61,
    62

Wanstead, 26–27, 28, 29,
    95
West, Benjamin, 83
William and Mary (king
    and queen of England),
    86–87, 92, 97

PICTURE CREDITS

Rebecca Stefoff is a freelance writer of biographies and other nonfiction works for young readers, including *Women Pioneers* (1996) and *Finding the Lost Cities* (1997). She has also served as the editorial director of Chelsea House's PLACES AND PEOPLES OF THE WORLD and LET'S DISCOVER CANADA series. A resident of Philadelphia for 19 years, she now lives in Portland, Oregon.

James Scott Brady serves on the board of trustees with the Center to Prevent Handgun Violence and is the Vice Chairman of the Brain Injury Foundation. Mr. Brady served as Assistant to the President and White House Press Secretary under President Ronald Reagan. He was severely injured in an assassination attempt on the president, but remained the White House Press Secretary until the end of the administration. Since leaving the White House, Mr. Brady has lobbied for stronger gun laws. In November 1993, President Bill Clinton signed the Brady Bill, a national law requiring a waiting period on handgun purchases and a background check on buyers.